CONTENTS

Page

List of abbreviations	4	LAY	88
Introduction	5	LEAVE	91
AGREE	9	LET	94
BACK	10	LOOK	96
BE	11	MAKE	102
BEAR	16	PASS	107
BLOW	17	PAY	109
BREAK	19	PULL	111
BRING	23	PUT	115
CALL	28	RUN	123
CARRY	30	SEE	130
CATCH	33	SET	132
CLEAR	34	SHOW	137
COME	35	STAND	139
CUT	41	TAKE	143
DO	45	THINK	151
DRAW	48	THROW	154
FALL	50	TURN	156
GET	53	WEAR	162
GIVE	62	WORK	164
GO	65	English Japanese	
HAND	74	Glossary	169
HANG	75		
HOLD	77		
KEEP	81		
KNOCK	85		

LIST OF ABBREVIATIONS　　　略　語　表

cf	=	compare	比較（参照）せよ
e.g.	=	for example	例えば
esp	=	especially	特に
etc	=	et cetera	その他
i.e.	=	that is	すなわち
imper	=	imperative	命令法
insep	=	inseparable	分離できない
neg	=	negative	否定
opp	=	opposite	反対
pass	=	passive	受身
sb	=	somebody	だれか
sep	=	separable	分離できる
sth	=	something	なにか、あるもの
usu	=	usually	通例
vi	=	intransitive verb	自動詞
vt	=	transitive verb	他動詞

INTRODUCTION

The structure of English is completely different from that of Japanese and to study English does present considerable problems to Japanese people, particularly in its colloquial use of verbs followed by prepositions or adverbial particles – the phrasal verb.

Everyday English has always relied heavily on such basic verbs as **put**, **take**, **get**, **make**, **bring** and **let**, and can form many combinations of these verbs with one or more prepositions or adverbial particles. These look deceptively easy to the foreigner at first sight, but their meanings can be radically different from what one might expect. Could anyone, for example, guess the meaning of such a phrase as '**put up with**', purely from its constituent words?

The aim of this book is to illustrate the different meanings in the context of a practical and representative selection of the most useful and widely used phrasal verbs – in both spoken and written English. It contains 44 sections, each devoted to a principal verb and the numerous combinations it can make with different prepositions or adverbial particles. Each phrasal verb is annotated grammatically* and accompanied by: (a) a definition written in straightforward English, (b) one or two examples to fix the context, (c) a word-for-word translation of the definition in Japanese, and (d) the equivalent Japanese word or phrase – which may not be a word-for-word translation of the verb or the definition – wherever one exists.

Completion exercises at the end of each section give student and teacher extra material to practise the correct and appropriate usage of these phrases. A key to these exercises is available to teachers from the publishers. Because a wide range of vocabulary is necessary to illustrate the full use of the phrasal verbs, an English–Japanese glossary has been provided at the back of the book. It contains 249 items, each with a Japanese translation and a page reference indicating the point where the word first appears with a specific meaning in the text.

English Phrasal Verbs in Japanese is designed to be of the maximum possible use, either in class or for private study, to Japanese students whose level ranges from Cambridge First Certificate class to Proficiency.

---

*See classification of verbs, p.8.

は　し　が　き

　英語の文章構成は、日本語のそれと大変違うので、日本人にとって非常に難しい。特に口語英語によく用いられている前置詞や副詞を後ろに伴って出てくる動詞、すなわち、句動詞の使い方である。

　日常英語では、絶えず put, take, make, bring, let, 等の基本的動詞が用いられるが、これらの動詞は一つあるいは二つ以上の前置詞か副詞と共に、さまざまな連結語ー「句動詞」ーを形成して表れる。　一見この句動詞の持つ意味はやさしいように思える、しかし、その本来の意味はなかなか想像も及ばないものである。　例えば、'put up with'という句の意味を、この構成されている一つ一つの語の意味から、推測することができるであろうか。

　本書は、話ことば・書きことばにおいて最も役立ち、広く使われている句動詞の中でも、特に、実用的で且つ代表的なものを選び出し、例文にそう入して、その文脈から、同じ句が用いられていてもそれぞれ違った意味内容を持っているということを明示している。　全部で４４項目あり、各項目には主要動詞と前置詞や副詞と組み合わさった句が配列されている。　各句動詞には簡単な文法注解が添えられており、 a・英語の同義語、 b・例文、 c・日本語の語義、 d・日本語訳（同義語や逐語訳にならない）等が加えられている。

　各項目の終わりには、句動詞が適切に使い分けられるかどうかを試す完成練習問題が設けられている。　これらの解答は教師用手引きとして出版社から入手できる。また、各句動詞を解明するために多数の単語が使われているので、巻末に英語ー日本語のグロッサリー（用語解説表）が加えられている。　このグロッサリーには、２４９の英語の単語があり、おのおのに日本語の語義とそのページ数が記されている。

'English Phrasal Verbs in Japanese' は Cambridge First Certificate から Proficiency の試験を目ざす日本の学生を対象に、大いに役立てるように編集された本である。

CLASSIFICATION OF VERBS

vi: Verbs belonging to this category are normally inseparable, though sometimes adverbs may come between the verb and the particle, e.g. 'The procession passed by '/' The procession passed slowly by'.

vt sep: If the object of a verb belonging to this category is a noun, then the particle may precede or follow the noun, e.g. 'The man took off his hat' or 'The man took his hat off'. However, if the object is a pronoun (e.g. it, him, us) then the particle *must* follow it: 'The man took it off'.

vt sep*: Verbs belonging to this category must always be separated, regardless of whether the object is a noun or a pronoun, e.g. 'The sooner we get this job over the better' and 'The sooner we get it over the better'.

vt insep: Verbs belonging to this category must always be inseparable, that is to say the particle(s) must follow the verb immediately, regardless of whether the object is a noun or a pronoun, e.g. 'The police are looking into the case'/'The police are looking into it' and 'I look forward to meeting John'/'I look forward to meeting him'.

*All English words in the text marked with an asterisk appear, with a translation into Japanese, in the English–Japanese glossary at the back of the book.

本書の英語の単語で、星印＊の付いているものはすべてその日本語の語義が、巻末の

英語―日本語グロッサリーに表記されている。

AGREE

agree to
vt insep

accept; consent to
受け入れる，同意する

I'm pleased to hear that you have finally *agreed to* our proposals.
Her parents just won't *agree to* her marrying a foreigner.

agree (up)on
vt insep

be unanimous about
(ある事に) 意見が一致する

Why can't you two ever *agree on* anything?
They agreed on the course of action to be taken.
Has the date for the next meeting been *agreed upon* yet?

agree with
1 *vt insep*

have the same opinion as
同意見である，同意する

I *agree with* everything you have said so far.
Many people did not *agree with* the speaker on the last point he made.
I'm afraid I can't *agree with* you in this matter.

agree with
2 *vt insep*

tally with; correspond with
符合する，一致する

His story doesn't quite *agree with* that of the other witness, does it?

agree with
3 *vt insep*

approve of
是認する，賛成する

Do you *agree with* nudity on the stage?
I don't *agree with* spoiling children too much.

agree with
4 *vt insep*

suit sb.'s health, temperament, etc.
合う

Indian food does not *agree with* me.
The tropical climate does not *agree with* David.

EXERCISE 1

Fill in the blank spaces with the correct prepositions:

1 The manager agreed with my request for a day off.
2 Oh, there is no doubt about that; I entirely agree on you.
3 We could not agree with a price for the house.
4 Garlic does not agree with my husband.
5 The engineers will call off their strike if the management agrees ... their demands.
6 Do you agree with women smoking in the street?
7 Have you agreed with the terms of the contract yet?

BACK

back away
vi

retreat; move back
（恐れたりきらったりして）後退する，
あとずさりする

She *backed away* nervously at the sight of the snake.
The child *backed away* from the angry dog.

back down
vi

abandon an opinion, a claim, etc.
取り消す，捨てる

At first he refused to comply* with the court order, but *backed down* when he realized he could be penalized* heavily.
He won't *back down* unless he is forced to do so.

back on to
vt insep

overlook from the back
後ろはすぐ。。。になっている

Their house *backs on to* Hyde Park.
The shop *backs on to* a railway station.

back out
vi

withdraw (from a promise, bargain, etc.)
取り消す

It's too late to *back out* now; I'm afraid we shall have to go through with it.
He *backed out* of the agreement, because he knew the others would not abide* by it.

back up
vt sep

give support to
支持する

If I protest against the decision, will you *back* me *up*?
The police were unwilling to believe her story, because she had no evidence to *back* it *up*.

EXERCISE 2

Fill in the blank spaces with the correct prepositions or particles:

1 He always backs his friends *up* when they are in trouble.
2 They have backed *out* the bargain at the last minute.
3 The house backs *on to* the football stadium.
4 He was quite determined to fight for it, but now he seems to have backed *down*
5 The frightened horses backed *away* from the tiger.

BE

be about to
vi

be on the point of
...しようとしている

The teacher *was about to* start the lesson when I came in.
The ceremony *is about to* finish.

be after
vt insep

want; seek
。。。がほしい，求める

He doesn't really love her; he's only *after* her money.
What *are* you *after*? Just tell me plainly.

be along
vi

come; arrive
来る，行く

The doctor will *be along* any minute now.
Tell Mr Hopkins I'll *be along* in a moment.

be away
vi

be absent (from home, office, etc.)
留守である，不在である

I'm afraid Mrs Thompson *is away* on holiday this week.
He's *away* from the office and won't be back till Thursday.

be back
vi

return; have returned
帰る

The manager is out for lunch. He'*ll be back* in an hour or so.
I'*ll be back* as soon as I can.

be behind
vi, vt insep

be late; be delayed
遅れている，後れている

They *were* well *behind* with the schedule.
We *are* all *behind* with our payments.
Suzy *is behind* the rest of the girls in her studies.

be down
vi

be depressed; be dejected
しょげている，（意気など）沈んでいる

Jonathan *is* a bit *down* because he failed his driving test.

be down on
vt insep

be prejudiced against; be critical of
...に偏見を持つ，批判的である

All the critics seem *to be down on* that author.
She *has been down on* him ever since he complained about her to the boss.

be for
vt insep

be in favour of
賛成する

I'*m for* the Republicans, but he'*s for* the Democrats.
Are you *for* or against the abolition* of the death* penalty?

be in
vi

be at home, in one's office, etc.
...に居る

I'd like to see Dr. Bentley. *Is* he *in*?
Yes, he'*s in*, but I'm afraid he's rather busy at the moment.

be off
1 *vi*

go; leave
行く，帰る

I'm sorry I can't keep the appointment with you; I'*m off* to Paris tomorrow.

	We'd better *be off* before it gets dark. I must *be off* now; it's getting rather late.
be off 2 *vi*	be cancelled 中止になる，延期になる
	The meeting which was scheduled for tomorrow *is off*. The match *is off* once again.
be off 3 *vi*	have gone bad (食べ物) いたんでいる
	The fish you've sold me *is off*. Don't eat that steak; it*'s* slightly *off*.
be on 1 *vi*	(of films etc.) be showing 上映中である，上演中である
	I wonder what film *is on* at the Imperial Cinema. 'Macbeth' *was on* at the Royal Theatre only last week.
be on 2 *vi*	be going to take place 催される，予定される
	The meeting *is on* again in spite of all the setbacks.
be out 1 *vi*	be out of the house, office, etc. 出ている
	The manager *is out* for lunch, but he'll be back at one o'clock.
be out 2 *vi*	be inaccurate; be wrong 不正確である，間違っている
	The doctor *was* way *out* in his diagnosis*. They *were* far *out* in their calculations.
be out 3 *vi*	be on strike ストライキをする
	The miners *are out* again. Most of the workers at that factory *were out* during the last two weeks.

be out of *vt insep*	have no more of 切らす

We *are out of* bread. Will you go and buy some?
The shops *are* completely *out of* milk.

be out to *vi*	be determined to ．．．する決心である

Robin *is* all *out to* pass his final examinations.
The government *is out to* curb inflation.

be over *vi*	be finished; be ended 終わる

The present heat wave is expected *to be over* soon.
Well, it*'s* all *over* now. You needn't worry about it any longer.

be through *vi*	reach the end of a relationship 縁が切れる

I won't put up with his bad temper any longer. We*'re through*.

be through with *vt insep*	be finished with 終える，仕上げる

I'll join you as soon as I*'m through with* these letters.
I don't know when he'll *be through with* that job.

be up 1 *vi*	be out of bed 起きる

The children *were up* at five this morning.
He must *be up* by now. It's nearly twelve o'clock.

be up 2 *vi*	(of time) expire; be finished 時間切れになる

Time*'s up*, gentlemen!
She managed to answer all the questions before the time *was up*.

be up to 1 *vt insep*	be capable of 。。。ができる	

He has made a terrible mess of the job. I'm afraid he *is* not *up to* it.
When she was younger, she *was up to* walking ten miles a day.

be up to 2 *vt insep*	be equal to 。。。に適している	

Your work *is* not *up to* the required standard.

be up to 3 *vt insep*	depend on 。。。しだいである，。。。の責任である	

You can either punish him or let him off. It's entirely *up to* you.
It's not *up to* me to decide on these matters.

be up to 4 *vt insep*	be engaged in (some mischievous act) (何かいたずらを) たくらむ	

These boys *are* always *up to* mischief.
Don't trust that fellow; I tell you he *is up to* no good.

EXERCISE 3

Fill in the blank spaces with the correct prepositions or particles:

1. Philip has been ill for well over a month. He must be ... with his studies by now.
2. The concert was ... at eleven o'clock.
3. What have you been ......? I haven't seen you for ages.
4. I'm ...... money at the moment. Will you lend me a few pounds?
5. What play is ... at the Shakespeare Theatre?
6. The delegation* is ... to Russia on a highly important mission.
7. We thought we would need ten bottles of wine for the party, but we were ... in our estimate. In fact we needed seven more.
8. The patient's condition has improved considerably, but he is not ... ... going out yet.
9. He has just gone to the shop to buy a few things, and will be ... in half an hour.
10. I was just ...... have my dinner when the telephone rang.
11. We are not going to do the show after all; it's ....

15

12 The choice is not entirely ...... me, I'm afraid. I'll have to consult my partner.
13 We should be ...... this job by Friday at the latest.
14 She was ... early this morning to do the packing.
15 You don't seem to be fond of Stuart. You're always ...... him.

BEAR

bear down (up)on
vt insep

move swiftly and menacingly towards
急に襲いかかる，．．．にぐんぐん近づく

A lion *was bearing down upon* its helpless prey* at lightning speed.
The big ship *bore down on* our small boat.

bear out
vt sep

confirm; support
確証する，支援する

This story of yours *bears out* his innocence beyond all doubt.
Is there anyone who can *bear* you *out* on this?
My friend Hill *will bear out* everything I have told you.

bear up
vi

remain strong under adversity or affliction
堪え忍ぶ，（失望しないで）がんばる

It must be very hard for her *to bear up* against the death of her only child.
I know how disappointed you must be feeling, but do try *to bear up*, won't you?

bear (up)on
vt insep

relate to; affect
．．．に関係がある，影響がある

How *does* this *bear on* the subject we are discussing?
These are major issues that directly *bear upon* the security of the state.

bear with
vt insep

tolerate; be patient with
許す，我慢する

I can't *bear with* his foul temper any longer.
If you *will bear with* me for a few more minutes, I will show you what I mean.
'*Bear with* me;
My heart is in the coffin there with Caesar,
And I must pause till it come back to me.'
                              Shakespeare, *Julius Caesar*

EXERCISE 4

Fill in the blank spaces with the correct prepositions or particles:

1 Your remark doesn't bear ... the matter at issue, I'm afraid.
2 The evidence you have now bears ... my theory.
3 How is she bearing ... after her bereavement*?
4 Bear ... me while I find the letter.
5 The headmistress bore ...... the frightened girls.
6 I find it impossible to bear ... his impudence*.
7 What you are telling me now bears ... my suspicions.

BLOW

blow in(to)
vi, vt insep

arrive unexpectedly
ひょっこり現れる

John *blew in* last night to tell us about his promotion.
Guess who*'s* just *blown into* my office.

blow out
vi, vt sep

be extinguished; extinguish
消える，吹き消す

The lamp *will blow out* if you don't shut that door.
The little girl was anxious *to blow out* the candles on her birthday cake.

blow over
vi

subside; be forgotten
(暴風などが) おさまる，忘れられる

The crew of the ship were greatly relieved when the storm finally *blew over*.
There is no need to worry about it; the whole thing *will* soon *blow over*.

blow up 1 *vi*	(of a storm etc.) develop （暴風などが）発生する	

If a storm were suddenly *to blow up*, our boat would capsize*.

blow up 2 *vi*	lose one's temper 怒り出す	

When the soldier refused to carry out his orders, the sergeant just *blew up*.
I'm sorry I *blew up* at you yesterday; I was in a rather bad mood.

blow up 3 *vi, vt sep*	(cause to) explode 爆発する，爆破する	

The bomb *blew up*, killing five people.
The commandos* *blew* the bridge *up* and fled unharmed.
A lot of oil refineries* *were blown up* during the last war.

blow up 4 *vt sep*	inflate; fill with air ふくらませる，空気を入れる	

The child kept *blowing up* the balloon till it burst.
Before you go on the road, make sure your tyres *are* properly *blown up*.

blow up 5 *vt sep*	reprimand; scold きびしくしかる	

The teacher *blew* me *up* for arriving late this morning.

blow up 6 *vt sep*	enlarge 引き伸ばす，大きくする	

Get someone *to blow up* these photographs, please.
I'd like you *to blow up* this part of the picture as much as you can.

EXERCISE 5

Use synonyms* in place of the underlined phrasal verbs:

1 The mother <u>blew</u> her son <u>up</u> for answering her back.

2 The much-talked-about scandal finally blew over.
3 Who do you think blew in to see me this morning?
4 We have enough explosives to blow up the entire building.
5 I thought I'd just blow in to see how you are getting on with your work.
6 The wind blew the light out.
7 He just blew up when I told him I'd forgotten to post the letter.
8 She liked the picture and wanted to have it blown up.

BREAK

break away 1 *vi*	secede 脱退する	

Several members of the Labour Party *have broken away* in protest against its nationalization policy.

break away 2 *vi*	renounce; abandon 。。。と手を切る，。。。と別れる	

It's not always easy *to break away* from bad company.
He *has broken away* from his family and decided to settle in Canada.

break away 3 *vi*	free oneself from 逃げる，離れる	

The prisoner managed *to break away* from his guards.

break down 1 *vi*	cease to function 故障する	

My car *has broken down* again and badly needs servicing. These machines *will break down* if they are left without proper maintenance.

break down 2 *vi*	be discontinued (交渉などが途中で) だめになる，中断する	

The negotiations *broke down* and may not be resumed* until the autumn.

break down 3 *vi*	break into tears; collapse 泣きくずれる，倒れる	

On hearing of her husband's death she *broke down*.
His health *has broken down* from overwork and malnutrition*.

break down 4 *vt sep*	destroy by breaking こわす	

I'm going *to break down* the door if you won't let me in.

break down 5 *vt sep*	classify 分析する，分類する	

If you *break* these statistics *down*, you'll see that 50% of those unemployed are under the age of twenty.

break in 1 *vt sep*	train (a horse etc.) しつける，訓練する	

It would be foolish of you to try to ride that vicious horse before it *is* safely *broken in*.

break in 2 *vi*	interrupt さえぎる，中断する	

A few hecklers* *broke in* as the minister was speaking.

break in(to) 1 *vi, vt insep*	force entry into 乱入する，押し入る	

Thieves *broke in* and ransacked* the house.
Burglars* *broke into* the museum and stole eight priceless paintings.

break into 2 *vt insep*	begin suddenly 急に。。。し始める	

On hearing the funny joke everyone *broke into* laughter.
As they boarded the bus, the boys *broke into* song.

break off 1 *vi*	stop for a rest or break 中断する，休憩する

The workers *broke off* for lunch at twelve.
Let us *break off* for just a few minutes.

break off 2 *vt sep*	terminate; sever (関係を）絶つ，やめる，切る

Unable to settle their differences, they decided *to break off* their engagement.
Many African countries *have broken off* diplomatic relations with Israel.

break off 3 *vt sep*	detach 割る，折る

The child *broke off* a piece of chocolate and gave it to his sister.

break out 1 *vi*	start suddenly 突然に起こる，発生する

The First World War *broke out* in 1914.
Fire *broke out* in the hotel and destroyed it completely.
A new epidemic* of cholera *has broken out*.

break out 2 *vi*	escape (from a place) 逃げ出す

If he tries *to break out* shoot him.
Three men *broke out* of this prison last week.

break through *vi, vt insep*	penetrate 突入する

After two weeks of dogged* fighting, our troops *broke through* (the enemy's lines).

break up 1 *vi*	disband (at the end of term) 休暇に入る

The school *breaks up* on June 18th.
When *do* you *break up* for the Christmas holidays?

break up
2 *vi, vt sep*

break into pieces
ばらばらになる，解体する

The ship *broke up* on the rocks.
We *broke up* the old car and sold it as scrap.

break up
3 *vi, vt sep*

disperse; scatter
解散する，追い散らす

The meeting *broke up* at about eleven.
The police used tear-gas *to break up* the demonstration.

break up
4 *vi*

(of a couple) part
別れる

I thought they were very happy together. Why *did* they *break up*?
Peter and Lily *broke up* nearly a year ago.

EXERCISE 6

Fill in the blank spaces with the correct prepositions or particles:
1. They suddenly broke ... their conversation when they saw me coming.
2. When do you break ... for Easter?
3. I want you to break ... these figures and tell me how much we have spent on housing schemes alone.
4. When did the Second World War break ... ?
5. The bus broke ... on the way to Glasgow, and we were stranded there for hours.
6. Will you please stop breaking ... while I'm talking!
7. When he learnt of his son's tragic death, the old man broke ... and cried.
8. During the recent riots many department stores were broken ... and looted*.
9. Fifty people were killed when a fire broke ... in the building.
10. During the American Civil War, eleven states broke ... to form the Southern Confederacy.
11. The prisoner broke ... of gaol by climbing a nine-foot wall.
12. Judith has broken ... her engagement to Anthony.
13. If we don't break ... the fight, someone will get hurt.
14. I tied the horse to a tree, but he managed to break ....
15. Someone broke ... my office and stole the papers.

BRING

bring about
vt sep
cause to happen
引き起こす，もたらす

We sincerely hope that these talks *will bring about* a reconciliation* between the two countries.
It was the Watergate affair that *brought about* the downfall of Richard Nixon.

bring back
1 *vt sep*
return
返す

I'll lend you my car provided you *bring* it *back* tomorrow.

bring back
2 *vt insep*
reintroduce
復活させる，再び導入する

A lot of M.P.'s* are clearly in favour of *bringing back* capital* punishment.

bring back
3 *vt sep*
recall to the mind; remind one of
思い出させる

That old song *brought back* happy memories to her.
It's amazing how a few words can *bring* it all *back*.

bring down
1 *vt sep*
shoot down (a plane)
撃墜する

Twenty of the enemy's fighter aircraft *have been brought down* by ground-to-air missiles.

bring down
2 *vt sep*
cause to fall
倒す

These unpopular measures could *bring* the government *down*.

bring down
3 *vt sep*
reduce; lower (a price)
（値段を）下げる

The government intends *to bring* the price of bread *down* to fifteen pence a loaf.

23

bring forth
vt insep

produce; yield
(作物が) できる、産する、もたらす

If the drought* continues to persist, the fruit-trees *will bring forth* nothing.
I wonder what the future *will bring forth*.

bring forward
1 *vt sep*

raise; propose for discussion
(案などを) 持ち出す、議題とする

I feel we ought *to bring forward* this proposal at the next meeting of the Council.

bring forward
2 *vt sep*

make earlier
繰り上げる

The committee has decided *to bring forward* the date of the conference to next May.
In view of this emergency, our meeting is *to be brought forward* from the 20th to the 13th April.

bring in
1 *vt sep*

introduce (a reform, a Bill*, etc.)
提出する、持ち出す

The Prime Minister intends *to bring in* major industrial reforms*.
The government is expected *to bring in* a Bill on road safety shortly.

bring in
2 *vt sep*

yield; produce
(利益、収入などを) もたらす

His investments in the various companies *bring* him *in* a total of £1000 a year.

bring in
3 *vt insep*

pronounce (a verdict)
評決を下す

The jury* *brought in* a verdict* of 'not guilty'.
To the great relief of the accused, a verdict of 'not guilty' *was brought in*.

bring off
1 *vt sep*

bring to a successful conclusion
見事にやってのける

The scheme will meet with strong opposition, but we believe we can *bring* it *off* eventually.

bring off
2 *vt sep*

rescue
救う

The coastguard patrol *brought off* the crew of the sinking ship.
All passengers *were brought off* by helicopters.

bring on
vt sep

cause; induce
起こす，招く

Such cold and extremely damp weather often *brings on* influenza.
Her attack of pneumonia* *was brought on* by the severe winter and lack of adequate heating at home.

bring out
1 *vt sep*

show; reveal; expose
示す，明らかにする

The teacher gave sentences *to bring out* the difference between 'destiny'* and 'destination'.
The inquiry may well *bring out* surprising things about the illicit* practices of some police officers.

bring out
2 *vt sep*

publish (see *come out* (3))
出版する

The publishers *have* just *brought out* a new edition of their popular cookery book.
His new novel *will be brought out* in a month's time.

bring over
vt sep

convince; convert
(。。。側に) 引き入れる，（別の考えに）変えさせる

We may be able *to bring* him *over* to our side, but it won't be easy.

bring round
1 *vt sep**

carry or take (to a certain place)
持ってくる，連れてくる

Tell the chauffeur *to bring* the car *round* to the front door.
Bring her *round* to see me one evening, won't you?

---

* Phrasal verbs which are marked *sep** must always be separated from their particles.

bring round 2 *vt sep**	restore to consciousness 意識を回復させる
	We *brought* him *round* by splashing cold water on his face. With the help of a doctor, it shouldn't take long *to bring* the young lady *round*.
bring round 3 *vt sep**	= bring over
bring through *vt sep**	save (a sick person) (病人を) 救う
	She was critically ill in hospital, but good doctors *brought* her *through*. Even the best medical treatment failed *to bring* the patient *through* his illness.
bring to *vt sep**	= BRING ROUND (2)
bring under *vt sep**	subdue; control 鎮圧する，．．．の下に支配する
	The rebels must *be brought under* at all costs. Germany *was brought under* Fascist rule.
bring up 1 *vt sep*	rear; raise 養う，育てる，しつける
	To *bring up* a family of six must cost a lot of money these days. Those children *are* very badly *brought up*. He *was brought up* to obey his elders and betters.
bring up 2 *vt sep*	vomit 吐く
	She was very ill and *brought up* everything she had eaten. The baby keeps *bringing up* her food.

bring up　　　　　raise; mention
3 *vt sep*　　　　　（話題，案などを）持ち出す，

　　　　　　　　　He promised *to bring* the matter *up* at the next committee meeting.
　　　　　　　　　Several interesting points *were brought up* in the course of the discussion.

EXERCISE 7

A Use synonyms in place of the underlined phrasal verbs:
1 New measures are being <u>brought in</u> to deal with tax* evasion.
2 I wish you'd stop <u>bringing up</u> this subject every time I see you.
3 The sudden outbreak of cholera has been <u>brought about</u> by the recent floods.
4 What verdict did the jury <u>bring in</u>?
5 When his mother died, Charles Dickens was <u>brought up</u> by his sister.
6 Living in such squalid* conditions <u>brings on</u> all kinds of diseases.
7 <u>Bring</u> the laundry <u>round</u> to my house.
8 I think they ought to <u>bring back</u> corporal* punishment.
9 Owing to the surplus of butter its price has been <u>brought down</u> considerably.
10 That publishing firm has <u>brought out</u> a new science encyclopaedia.

B Fill in the blank spaces with the correct prepositions or particles. In some examples more than one answer is possible:
1 It shouldn't be difficult to bring him ... to our way of thinking.
2 He was badly injured in a car accident, but special attention and good nursing brought him ....
3 A reconnaissance* plane was brought ... by anti-aircraft artillery*.
4 These new products bring ... a good deal of money.
5 We are bringing ... his collection of essays next month.
6 New land is being brought ... cultivation.
7 She fainted in a crowded bus, but was quickly brought ... with a brandy.
8 Please bring the book ... to me when you've finished with it.
9 They have brought ... yet another important business deal.
10 The MP was so concerned about the matter that he intended to bring it ... in Parliament.

27

CALL

call back
1 *vi, vt sep*

telephone back
（電話をかけてきた人に）あとで電話する

The operator *called back* while you were out.
I'*ll call* you *back* as soon as I know the results.

call back
2 *vt sep*

recall; summon to return
召還する，呼びもどす

The ambassador *has been called back* for urgent consultations with his government.

call for
1 *vt insep*

require; demand
要する，要求する

Such delicate matters *call for* considerable tact and skill.
The good news *calls for* a celebration.
The Home* Secretary *is calling for* an inquiry into allegations* of corruption* in the police department.

call for
2 *vt insep*

go and fetch
迎えに行く，取りに行く

I'*ll call for* you at your office at, say, four o'clock.
He said he *would call for* his car tomorrow afternoon.

call forth
vt insep

bring into action; provoke
よび起こす

This crisis *has called forth* all his energy.
The government's decision *has called forth* angry protests from Labour back-benchers*.

call in
1 *vt sep*

summon to a place
呼ぶ，...の援助を求める

We can't afford *to call in* a technician every time the TV set breaks down.
She *has called* her lawyer *in* and instructed him to draw up a new will.

call in 2 *vt sep*		request the return of 回収する，取り立てる，集める
		The manufacturers *have called in* all the defective* models and corrected them. The firm will soon start *calling* their debts *in*.
call off *vt sep*		cancel; abandon 中止する，取り消す，やめる
		We had *to call off* the procession* because of the bad weather. They *called* the deal *off* at the very last minute. The search for the missing aircraft *was* finally *called off*.
call out 1 *vt sep*		announce in a loud voice 読み上げる
		Will you please keep quiet while I *call out* the results. The teacher *called out* the names of the pupils before starting the lesson.
call out 2 *vt sep*		summon to strike （召集して）ストに駆り出す，ストをさせる
		Following their abortive* talks with the government, the Union officials decided *to call* the workers *out*.
call up 1 *vt sep*		telephone; ring up 電話する
		I'*ll call* you *up* as soon as I get there. David *called* me *up* last night and told me about the accident.
call up 2 *vt sep*		summon for military service 召集する
		The army *is calling up* reservists* in case of renewed hostilities. He *was called up* just before the outbreak of the war.

call (up)on 1 *vt insep*	visit briefly ちょっと訪ねる While I was in London I *called on* aunt Felicity. I will *call on* you at about five, if that is convenient for you.
call (up)on 2 *vt insep*	invite; request 。。。するように言う，頼む I will now *call on* Mr Jones to deliver his speech. The secretary was *called upon* to read the minutes* of the meeting.

EXERCISE 8

Fill in the blank spaces with the correct prepositions or particles:

1 The football pitch was so wet that the referee decided to call ... the match.
2 Here is my phone number; you can call me ... any time between 8 am and 4 pm.
3 The library is calling ... all the books that are overdue*.
4 When I went to Italy last year I called ... my friends in Rome.
5 You look very ill. Shall I call ... a doctor?
6 He has been called ... from Berlin to supervise the operation.
7 This alarming situation calls ... immediate action.
8 She stepped forward to receive her prize when her name was called ...
9 Harry is calling ... me at seven to take me to the pictures.
10 He was never called ... to the army because of his poor healtn.

CARRY

carry away *vt sep*	(*usu. pass.*) deprive of self-control 夢中になる，興奮する The speaker got *carried away* by his enthusiasm*. She was so *carried away* by her emotions that she did not know what she was saying. We haven't won the game yet, so don't get *carried away*.

carry forward　　transfer (an amount etc.) to the next column, page, etc.
　vt sep　　次の欄，ページに繰り越す

　　　　　　　　　The book-keeper *carried* the figures *forward* to the next page.
　　　　　　　　　At the end of the month all balances *are carried forward*.

carry off　　handle
　1 *vt sep**　　取り扱う，処理する

　　　　　　　　　She had a difficult part to play, but she *carried* it *off* extremely well.

carry off　　win (a prize etc.)
　2 *vt sep*　　獲得する

　　　　　　　　　The Russian athletes *carried off* most of the gold medals at the last Olympic Games.
　　　　　　　　　Who do you think *will carry off* the first prize in tomorrow's competition?

carry on　　continue; proceed
　1 *vi*　　続ける

　　　　　　　　　She was asked to stop talking and *carry on* with her work.
　　　　　　　　　Sorry if I interrupted you. Please *carry on*!
　　　　　　　　　I tried to start a conversation with him, but he just ignored me and *carried on* reading his paper.

carry on　　have an affair (with)
　2 *vi*　　(．．．と) 浮気をする

　　　　　　　　　They *had been carrying on* for quite a while, but managed to keep it secret.
　　　　　　　　　All the neighbours know that his wife *is carrying on* with the lodger.

carry on　　behave
　3 *vi*　　振舞う

　　　　　　　　　If you *carry on* in that way, you'll get yourself a bad name.

carry on 4 *vt insep*	manage (a business) 経営する	

His father *carries on* a textile business in the centre of town.

carry on 5 *vt insep*	hold (a conversation) (会話を) する，続ける	

It's impossible *to carry on* any kind of conversation in this terrible noise.

carry out *vt insep*	execute; perform 実行する，果たす，する	

A plan such as this would be very costly *to carry out*.
They *did* not *carry out* their promise to help us.
The doctor's orders will have *to be carried out* to the letter.

carry through 1 *vt sep*	accomplish; complete 完成する，遂行する	

We did not have enough capital *to carry* the scheme *through*.
The enterprise *was carried through* in spite of all the setbacks.

carry through 2 *vt sep**	help through a difficult period 切り抜ける，がんばり抜く	

His dogged determination did not fail *to carry* him *through*.
They prayed to God *to carry* them *through* their ordeal*.

EXERCISE 9

Fill in the blank spaces with the correct particles:

1 An extensive search for the missing aeroplane is being carried ... by rescue teams.
2 The teacher read the first paragraph and then asked Helen to carry ....
3 If we are to win the war, our struggle must be carried ... to the end.
4 She suspected that her husband was carrying ... with the woman next door.
5 Every time we discuss our holiday plans, my wife just gets carried ....
6 The Belgian team carried ... all the trophies at the show-jumping event.
7 Their son carries ... the business of a hotelier at a seaside resort .
8 He carried ... like a child at the party.

CATCH

catch on
1 *vi*

become popular
人気を得る，ヒットする

The latest Paris fashions *have caught on* rapidly everywhere in Europe.
This kind of song is likely *to catch on* with the younger generation.

catch on
2 *vi*

understand; comprehend
理解する

She is a very shrewd woman. Trust her *to catch on* to what they are doing.

catch out
vt sep*

trap; trick
引っかける

Are you trying *to catch* me *out* with these smart questions of yours?
You'd better be careful with him, or he'*ll catch* you *out*.

catch up (with)
vi, vt sep*

draw level with
．．．に追いつく

He was unable *to catch up* with the rest of the class, because of his repeated absence from school.
We have to run faster, or they'*ll* soon *catch* us *up*.

EXERCISE 10

Fill in the blank spaces with the correct particles:

1 Vera has been ill for some time now. It'll take her a few weeks to catch ... with her work.
2 These revolutionary ideas will never catch ... in a conservative society such as ours.
3 They left only a few minutes ago, but if you hurry you should be able to catch ... with them.
4 Do you think this new style will ever catch ... ?
5 It's no good trying to catch me .... I know all your little tricks.
6 He is no fool. Actually he's very quick at catching ....

CLEAR

clear away
1 *vi*

disappear; vanish
消える

The clouds are beginning *to clear away*.
The mist *will have cleared away* by the time we get there.

clear away
2 *vt sep*

remove
片付ける

When we had finished eating, the waitress *cleared away* the dirty plates.
The workers started *clearing* the debris* *away* shortly after the explosion.

clear off
1 *vi*

go away
出かける，どこかへ消える

You'd better *clear off* before my father arrives.
I don't want your help, so *clear off*!
Clear off, the lot of you!

clear off
2 *vt sep*

get rid of; dispose of
(借金などを) 支払う，始末する

He had accumulated so many debts that he could not *clear* them *off*.
If you intend *to clear off* this old stock you'll have to sell it cheaply.

clear out
1 *vi*

= CLEAR OFF (1)

clear out
2 *vt sep*

clean out; empty
空にする

She *cleared out* one of the cupboards to let her roommate use it.

clear out
3 *vt sep*

throw out; expel
追い出す

Go and *clear* those kids *out* of my room.
He *was cleared out* of the pub for causing a disturbance.

clear up 1 *vi*	(of the weather) become clear 晴れる

I hope the weather *will* soon *clear up*.
It's rather cloudy now, but it may *clear up* later in the day.

clear up 2 *vt sep*	make tidy; remove きれいに片付ける

She spent all morning *clearing up* the children's playroom.
After the party, some guests stayed behind to help *clear up* the mess.

clear up 3 *vt sep*	make clear, solve 明らかにする，解決する，解く

Before we go any further, I'd like *to clear up* this matter once and for all.
The mystery of the kidnapped heiress* *was* never *cleared up*.

EXERCISE 11

Use synonyms in place of the underlined phrasal verbs:

1 The gang cleared off when they saw the police coming.
2 We were so glad to see the clouds clearing away.
3 I'll clear out this desk for you, and you can put your things in it.
4 We waited for the weather to clear up before we resumed our march.
5 You've got no right to hunt on my land, so clear off.
6 Who is going to clear up this rubbish?
7 We still have this point to clear up before we can go on to consider the next one.
8 Having finished eating our lunch, we cleared away the dishes.

COME

come about *vi*	happen; arise 起こる，生じる

Their quarrel *came about* through a slight misunderstanding.
How *does* it *come about* that he has lost three jobs in as many months?

35

come across *vt insep*	meet or find by chance 。。。に (偶然) 出くわす，見つける	

I *came across* an old school friend while on holiday in France.
Where *did* you *come across* this necklace?

come at 1 *vt insep*	reach; arrive at (see 'get at' (2)) 。。。に至る，達する，。。。を得る	

The truth is often difficult *to come at*.
The purpose of this investigation is *to come at* the true facts of the case.

come at 2 *vt insep*	attack; assault 襲う，。。。に向って来る	

The man *came at* me with a big knife.

come back *vi*	return 帰る	

Her husband went away and never *came back*.
I'*ll come back* as soon as I can manage it.

come by *vt insep*	obtain 手に入れる	

How *did* you *come by* these foreign coins?
Jobs such as these are not easy *to come by* these days.

come down 1 *vi*	fall; become cheaper 下がる	

The price of bread is expected *to come down* soon.
The cost of living is always going up; it never *comes down*.

come down 2 *vi*	lower oneself 落ちぶれて。。。するようになる	

She *has come down* to asking for money.
I never thought he *would come down* to begging for work.

come down on *vt insep*	scold; punish どなりつける，罰する
	The headmaster *came down on* me like a ton of bricks. The government intends *to come down* heavily *on* draft* dodgers.
come in 1 *vi*	enter 入る
	I knocked on the door and was asked *to come in*. *Come in*, please!
come in 2 *vi*	become fashionable 流行する，はやる
	Mini skirts *are coming in* again after having been out of fashion for some years. Long hair first *came in*, in the early sixties.
come in 3 *vi*	gain power; be elected (see *get in* (2)) 当選する
	Had the Socialists *come in* they would probably have taken tougher measures against inflation. When the Labour government *came in*, the country was already in a difficult financial situation.
come into *vt insep*	inherit (財産，権利などを）受け継ぐ
	He *came into* a large sum of money when his uncle died. She has deserted most of her old acquaintances since she *came into* a fortune.
come off 1 *vi*	become detached とれる，抜ける
	Two of the buttons on my new shirt *have come off*. The handle *came off* when she lifted the tea-pot.
come off 2 *vi*	take place 行われる
	When does the wedding *come off*? Her proposed visit to France never *came off*. Steve's birthday party *came off* very well indeed.

come off 3 *vi*	be successful 成功する，うまくいく His attempt to persuade the manager to give him a pay rise *did* not *come off*.
come on 1 *vi*	progress; develop 進む，進歩する，成長する How's Freddy *coming on* in his new job? The roses *are coming on* well.
come on 2 *vi*	begin; arrive やってくる，降り出す，近付く Winter *came on* rather late this year. The rain *came on* quite unexpectedly, and we were all drenched*. We managed to reach the village before darkness *came on*.
come on 3 *vi*	(*imper.*) hurry up (懇願などを表わして) さあ早く早く *Come on*, girls! We are going to be late for the party. Oh, *do come on*!
come out 1 *vi*	blossom 花が咲く，（芽が）出る The garden grew more and more colourful as the flowers *were coming out*. When *do* the buds *come out*?
come out 2 *vi*	appear; become visible 現れる，出てくる He likes to watch the stars *come out* at night. The sun *came out* in the early afternoon.
come out 3 *vi*	be published (see *bring out* (2)) 出版される，発行される His new book *will come out* in about two weeks' time. This fashion magazine *comes out* every fortnight.

come out 4 *vi*	be revealed; become known 明らかになる，知られる
	The truth about his criminal past eventually *came out*. Their secret is bound *to come out* sooner or later. When it *came out* that he had been involved in the scandal, he resigned his office*.
come out 5 *vi*	(of stains etc.) disappear (しみなどが) とれる
	I twice washed the table-cloth, but the stains *would* not *come out*.
come out with *vi insep*	say; utter 言う，述べる
	Every time I ask him about something, he *comes out with* some funny answers. She *came out with* a long story to explain why she did not turn up for work.
come over *vt insep*	seize; take possession of ．．．は．．．に襲われる
	Panic *came over* the passengers of the sinking ship. What *has come over* you that you behave so irrationally?
come round 1 *vi*	visit casually ぶらりとやって来る
	You can *come round* any time you like. We'll always be delighted to see you. Why *don't* you *come round* for a drink this evening?
come round 2 *vi*	regain consciousness (気絶した者が) 意識を回復する
	If she *doesn't come round* soon I'm going to call for an ambulance. How long was the old lady unconscious before she *came round*?

come round to
vt insep

adopt; accept
(意見を変えて人の考えに) 同調する

One day you'*ll come round to* my way of thinking.
He *came round to* our point of view when he realized we were right.

come through
vi, vt insep

survive; recover from
切り抜ける，回復する

The explorers *came through* many ordeals.
I'm glad to hear that Arthur *has come through* (his illness).

come to
1 *vi*

= COME ROUND (2)

come to
2 *vt insep*

amount to; total
。。。の額になる

The money he spends on clothes *comes to* £50 a month.
I didn't think the electricity bill *would come to* so much.

come under
vt insep

be classified under
。。。の部類に（項目に）入る

Books on animals *come under* 'zoology' in this catalogue.
What heading *does* this article *come under*?

come up
1 *vi*

arise; present itself
現われる

I haven't been able to find a job yet, but I hope something *will come up* soon.

come up
2 *vi*

be presented for discussion
(話，議論などに) 出る

The question of finance keeps *coming up* at every meeting of the board.

come up to
vt insep

equal; match
(期待に) 添う，(標準に) かなう

The results *did not come up to* our expectations.
His work *doesn't come up to* the required standard.

come up with
vt insep

offer; produce
提案する，考え出す

He *came up with* some good suggestions to improve working conditions at the factory.
I don't suppose Edward *will come up with* any sparkling ideas, do you?

EXERCISE 12

A Fill in the blank spaces with the correct prepositions or particles:

1 When I slammed the door, the handle came *off* in my hand.
2 The fog was gradually disappearing, and the sun was coming *out*.
3 I came *across* your cousin in the Tube* yesterday.
4 Many problems have come *out* in the course of the discussions.
5 The whole truth came *out* at the trial.
6 The sergeant came ...... the soldier who was caught napping*.
7 He came ...... the shocking news that Angela had committed suicide.
8 We have come *down* worse crises than this one.
9 The money she spends on food alone comes *to* £25 a week.
10 Have you ever come ... the word 'ornithology'*?

B Answer the following questions, using phrasal verbs with *come*:

1 How did he spend the money he *inherited* under his father's will? *come into*
2 When does the price of fruit usually *drop*? *come down*
3 Did the film you saw the other day *match* your expectations? *come up to*
4 How did the accident *happen*? *come off*
5 How is the new-born baby *progressing*? *come on*
6 Do you remember when the bikini first *became fashionable*? *come in*
7 Which political party *gained power* at the last general election? *come in*
8 In which month do daffodils normally *blossom*? *come out*
9 When did you *return* from your holiday abroad? *come back*
10 How did he *obtain* all this money? *come by*

CUT

cut away
vt sep

remove by cutting
切りとる

The gardener *cut away* the old branches from the trees.
The surgeon* *cut away* the diseased tissue* with infinite precision.*

cut back 1 *vt sep*	reduce 減らす，削減する	

Owing to a sharp slump in business, the management decided *to cut back* production by 15%.

cut back 2 *vt sep*	prune; cut 短く摘み込む，せん定する	

The gardener *cuts* the hedge *back* two or three times a year.
Those rose-bushes ought *to be cut back* more often.

cut down 1 *vt sep*	fell (a tree etc.) （木を）伐り倒す	

It would be a great pity if these trees were *to be cut down*.

cut down 2 *vt sep*	curtail; reduce （量を）減らす，切り詰める	

The doctor advised his patient *to cut down* smoking.
If prices continue to go up at this rate, we'll have *to cut down* our expenses.

cut down on *vt insep*	consume less of 減らす	

You must *cut down on* rich* food if you want to lose weight.
During the energy crisis, a lot of factories had *to cut down on* fuel.

cut in *vi*	interrupt さえぎる，割り込む	

Will you please stop *cutting in* while I'm talking!
Don't *cut in* so rudely – let him finish what he wants to say.

cut off 1 *vt sep*	sever 切る，切断する	

They have threatened *to cut off* the heads of the hostages if the ransom is not paid promptly.
Be careful that you *don't cut* your fingers *off*!

cut off
2 *vt sep*

isolate
孤立状態にする

A whole regiment* *was cut off* by the enemy and was forced to surrender*.
The villagers *were cut off* by the floods for nearly two weeks.

cut off
3 *vt sep*

disconnect
切る，止める

The Company *has cut off* our gas supply.
He was very annoyed when he *was cut off* in the middle of his phone call.

cut out
1 *vt sep*

extract or shape by cutting
切り抜く，裁断する

She *cut out* some pictures from the magazine and pinned them to the wall.
The tailor *cut out* a suit from the roll of cloth.

cut out
2 *vt sep*

stop; cease
よす，やめる

Why *don't* you *cut out* all this nonsense and listen to me for a change?
I'm sick and tired of your moaning*. Just *cut it out*, will you?

cut out
3 *vt sep*

(*usu. pass.*) be suited for
適している，．．．に向いている．

That young lady *is cut out* to be a teacher.
I really don't think I'm *cut out* for this sort of work.
William and Elizabeth seem *to be cut out* for each other.

cut out
4 *vt sep*

leave out; omit
取り除く，省く

If you intend to have your book published you will have *to cut out* all the rude words.

cut out 5 *vt sep*	stop; refrain from やめる，控える，我慢する	

Though his health was rapidly deteriorating* he could not *cut out* drinking.

cut up 1 *vt sep*	cut into pieces 切り分ける	

The butcher *cut up* the cow he had slaughtered.
The mother *cut* the cake *up* and gave the children a piece each.

cut up 2 *vt sep*	distress; upset 悲しませる，．。。の心を傷つける	

The news of her husband's death *cut* her *up* quite badly.
I *was* very *cut up* when I learned that Jennifer had broken her leg.

cut up 3 *vt sep*	criticise; attack 酷評する，さんざんにやっつける	

His latest book *has been* mercilessly *cut up* by the reviewers*.

EXERCISE 13

Use synonyms in place of the underlined phrasal verbs:

1 They will cut off our electricity supply if we don't pay the bill.
2 The seamstress* cut out a dress and started sewing it.
3 It is very impolite to cut in while others are speaking.
4 She cut the meat up with a sharp knife.
5 However hard he tried he could not cut out smoking.
6 We are using too much electricity; we shall have to cut down on it.
7 I feel completely cut off from the outside world.
8 She was very cut up at the news of her friend's death.
9 I can't see him as a lawyer; he doesn't seem to be cut out for that profession.
10 This article is far too long; you should cut out one or two paragraphs.

DO

do away with abolish; get rid of
1 *vt insep* 廃止（排除）する

Most countries in Europe *have done away with* capital punishment.
It's about time these old-fashioned customs *were done away with*.

do away with kill; murder
2 *vt insep* 殺す

The criminals *did away with* the witness who gave evidence against them.

do by treat
vt insep 。。。によくする

A good boss is one who always *does* well *by* his employees.
Do as you *would be done by*. (proverb)

do down disparage; speak ill of
1 *vt sep* けなす，（人を）悪く言う

He's always *doing* his colleagues *down* in public.

do down cheat; get the better of
2 *vt sep* だます

The salesman *did* her *down* over the price of her coat.
He's the kind of man who *would do* his own mother *down*.

do for help, usu. with housework
1 *vt insep* 。。。の身のまわりの世話をする

Mrs. Smith *has been doing for* him since his wife died.

do for (*usu. pass.*) ruin; finish off
2 *vt insep* 破壊する，荒廃する，おしまいにする，命を奪う

The country *was done for* after the earthquakes.
The old man had been ailing for some time, but it was pneumonia that finally *did for* him.

45

do in 1 *vt sep*	kill; murder 殺す	

You'd better keep an eye on this prisoner, or he'*ll do* somebody *in* one of these days.
She is not the first girl *to be done in* by this murderer.

do in 2 *vt sep*	(*pass.*) tired; exhausted 疲れる	

What's the matter, Tim? You look completely *done in*.
The housewife felt *done in* after the morning's work.

do out *vt sep*	clean or clear out 掃除する，整理する	

While you *do out* the cellar, I'll tidy up the living-room.
That cupboard *has not been done out* for months.

do out of *vt sep**	cheat (sb.) out of だまして...を取る	

He took advantage of her naivety* and *did* her *out of* a large sum of money.
The shopkeeper *did* me *out of* 50 pence.

do up 1 *vt sep*	renovate; modernize 手入れをする，修繕する	

The landlord *did up* all the rooms in the house before letting them out.
How much do you think it is going to cost us *to do up* the bathroom?

do up 2 *vt sep*	fasten; button (ボタン，フアスナー，ひもなどを) かける	

Hang on a minute while I *do up* my shoelaces*.
Could you *do* my dress *up* at the back, please?

do up 3 *vt sep*	make into a parcel 包む	

The girl at the counter *will do up* the books for you.
The presents *were done up* in lovely green paper.

do with 1 *vt insep*	(with 'can' or 'could') need 欲しい，．．．が必要である
	He said he could *do with* a new pair of shoes. Your shirt can *do with* a good wash. It looks absolutely filthy. We could *do with* a new vacuum* cleaner in this place.
do with 2 *vt insep*	be content with ．．．で間に合わせる，．．．で満足する
	Until we find a better place to live in we shall have *to do with* this small flat.
do with 3 *vt insep*	be related to; be connected with ．．．に関係がある，．．．にかかわる
	I don't know exactly what sort of job he has, but it is *to do with* computers. She's very interested in anything *to do with* Roman art.
do with 4 *vt insep*	(with *have*) have dealings with; be involved in ．．．と（に）関係がある，つきあい（取引）た
	I have nothing whatever *to do with* these men. We have reason to believe that he has something *to do with* the bank raid.
do without *vt insep*	manage without ．．．がなくてもいい，．．．を必要としない
	Children can't *do without* the help of their parents. Surely the country can *do without* fanatics* like you.

EXERCISE 14

Fill in the blank spaces with the correct prepositions or particles:

1 I could do ... a nice long holiday.
2 Every summer he and his wife do ... their house.
3 The government is planning to do ...... some outdated* laws.
4 He is thinking of selling his car, but he's not sure if he'll be able to do ... it.
5 She does ... the Pearsons three mornings a week.
6 What you've just said has nothing to do ... the subject under discussion.

7 She spent all the morning doing ... the attic.
8 She did ...... her husband by poisoning his food.
9 He was a blackmailer who deserved to be done ....
10 His employer did him ... ... his holiday pay.

DRAW

draw in　　　(of days) become shorter
1 *vi*　　　　　（日が）短くなる

　　　　　　　The days *are drawing in* as autumn approaches.

draw in　　　involve
2 *vt sep*　　　引きずり込む，巻き込む

　　　　　　　She strongly objected to their evil plans and would not let herself *be drawn in*.

draw in　　　attract
3 *vt sep*　　　引き寄せる，集める

　　　　　　　The new play *is drawing in* large audiences every night.

draw on　　　approach; come closer
vi　　　　　近づく，迫る

　　　　　　　As the date of the examination *drew on*, the candidates grew more and more tense.
　　　　　　　As winter *drew on*, they started preparing themselves for the cold months ahead.

draw out　　(of days) become longer
1 *vi*　　　　　（日が）次第に長くなる

　　　　　　　The days *are drawing out* as spring approaches.

draw out　　get sb to talk
2 *vt sep**　　...にしゃべらせる

　　　　　　　We tried to be friendly with the girl, but she was too shy *to be drawn out*.
　　　　　　　He's that quiet type of person who needs *to be drawn out*.

draw out
3 *vt sep*

prolong
だらだらと長く続ける

This debate* *has been drawn out* long enough.
You *have drawn out* your essay too much. Next time try to make it brief.

draw up
1 *vi*

come to a halt; stop
止まる

The bus *drew up* at the zebra* crossing.
The car *drew up* when the traffic lights changed to red.

draw up
2 *vt sep*

prepare; draft
作成する

She instructed her lawyer *to draw up* a new will.
The contract *was drawn up* in the presence of two witnesses.

draw up
3 *vt sep*

set in line
整列させる

The officer *drew up* his men before the parade started.
The soldiers *were drawn up*, ready for inspection.

EXERCISE 15

Fill in the blank spaces with the correct particles:

1 The days begin to draw ... after 21st December.
2 She has a gift of drawing ... even the most reserved* of people.
3 The taxi drew ... outside the hotel.
4 He refused to be drawn ... when the quarrel started.
5 The solicitor promised to draw ... the agreement in a day or two.
6 The days begin to draw ... after 21st June.

FALL

fall apart
vi
disintegrate; fall to pieces
崩壊する，だめになる

The house *is* practically *falling apart* and badly needs renovating*.
His whole life *has fallen apart* since his wife divorced him.

fall back
vi
retreat; withdraw
後退する，退却する

As the enemy troops advanced we *fell back*.
The defeated army *fell back* in utter disarray*.

fall back on
vt insep
have recourse to
頼る

It's always good to have a friend *to fall back on*.
If the worst comes to the worst we can *fall back on* mother to lend us the money.

fall behind
vi, vt insep
slacken in pace or progress
遅れる，追い抜かれる

Several of the runners *fell behind* in the Marathon.
Lazy students invariably *fall behind* the others (in their work).

fall behind with
vi
be late in/with
滞納する

He *fell behind with* his instalments* on the car.
She *has fallen behind with* the payments on the washing-machine.

fall down
vi
fall to the ground
。。。から落ちる

She *fell down* the stairs and broke her arm.
Jack *fell down* from the tree he was climbing.

fall for 1 *vt insep*	fall in love with 。。。にほれ込む，。。。が好きになる	

I *fell for* that girl the first time we met.
She *has fallen for* that young man in a big way.

fall for 2 *vt insep*	be deceived by だまされる	

I never thought you *would fall for* that old trick.
Every girl seems *to fall for* his smooth talk.

fall in 1 *vi*	collapse; give way つぶれる，くずれる	

The roof of the old tunnel could *fall in* any time.
The walls of the house *have fallen in*.

fall in 2 *vi*	get into line 整列する	

The sergeant ordered the soldiers *to fall in*.
Fall in!

fall in with 1 *vt insep*	meet by chance 偶然出会う	

In their journey through the desert they *fell in with* a party of nomads*.

fall in with 2 *vt insep*	agree to; concur with 同意する	

He says he is quite willing *to fall in with* the scheme.
They have finally *fallen in with* our proposals.

fall off 1 *vi*	diminish; dwindle 減る，だんだん小さくなる	

Our exports *have fallen off* appreciably* this year.
'Love cools, friendship *falls off*, brothers divide.'
　　　　　　　　　　　　Shakespeare, *King Lear*.

fall off 2 *vi*	deteriorate; worsen 悪くなる
	The service at that hotel *has fallen off* since it came under new management.
fall out 1 *vi*	happen; occur 起こる，生じる
	Everything *fell out* just as we had anticipated*. It *fell out* that nobody was in the house the night she was murdered.
fall out 2 *vi*	quarrel; disagree 争う，仲たがいする
	She *has fallen out* with her sister over some trivial matter. When thieves fall out honest men get their own. (proverb)
fall out 3 *vi*	opp. fall in (2) 開散する
fall through *vi*	miscarry; fail 失敗する，だめになる
	Their plans for starting a language school *fell through* for lack of capital. No one supported the scheme and it *fell through*.
fall to *vt insep*	start; begin 始める，．．．し始める
	No sooner had they got home than they *fell to* bickering*. He *fell to* wondering what to do with himself.
fall under *vt insep*	be classified under ．．．に入る，．．．に該当する
	Which heading *does* this item *fall under*? It *falls under* (the heading of) 'petty* cash'.

fall (up) on *vt insep*	attack; assault 攻撃する，襲う

The bandits* *fell on* the convoy* at sunset.
Enemy troops *fell upon* us from all directions.

EXERCISE 16

Fill in the blank spaces with the correct prepositions or particles:

1 The quality of the goods we now receive has fallen . . . . It is not what it used to be.
2 I'm afraid I can't manage the meeting tonight, but I'll fall . . . . . . whatever decisions you take.
3 As fresh fruit was not available we had to fall . . . . . . tinned fruit.
4 I'm sorry to hear that Anthony and Edward have fallen . . . They were such good friends.
5 She fell . . . from the roof and broke her neck.
6 He fell . . . that girl as soon as he saw her.
7 Attendance at these classes has fallen . . . since the new teacher took over.
8 He fell . . . with the rent when he was out of work.
9 We fell . . . . . . some interesting people from Mexico while on holiday in Spain.
10 It fell . . . that I was passing by when I heard the woman screaming.
11 The project to build a new sports centre has fallen . . . for lack of adequate* funds.
12 The old shed fell . . . during last night's gale.

GET

get about 1 *vi*	move about; travel あちこち出歩く，旅行する

Since he broke his leg he is finding it hard to *get about*.
Nowadays people *get about* much more than they used to.

get about 2 *vi*	spread; become known 広まる，知れ渡る	

It *got about* that she was having an affair* with the postman.
The news *got about* that he was emigrating to Canada.
A rumour *got about* that the wedding had been cancelled.

get across *vt sep**	convey; communicate （考え，情報などを）わからせる，理解させる	

He may be a very competent scientist, but he's certainly poor at *getting* his stuff* *across* (to the class).
The speaker was trying hard *to get* his point *across* (to his audience).

get ahead *vi*	pass beyond; progress 。。。を追い抜く，成功する，	

Francis *got ahead* of the runners in the race.
I'm pleased to hear that we *are getting ahead* with the project after all.

get along 1 *vi*	go; depart 行く，出掛ける	

We'd better be *getting along* before it starts raining.
Well, I must be *getting along* now. It's nearly one o'clock.

get along (with) 2 *vi*	progress はかどる，進める	

How *are* you *getting along* with your French lessons?
We *are getting along* well with the job.

get along 3 *vi*	manage 暮らす，（うまく）やっていく	

I don't know how you expect me *to get along* without money.
You shouldn't worry too much about us. We'*ll get along* somehow.

get along
4 *vi*

be on good terms (with)
仲よく暮していく，折り合う

Judith and her room-mate do not seem *to get along* well together.
It's very easy *to get along* with the new boss; he's a most charming man.

get at
1 *vt insep*

reach
届く

She placed the books on the top shelf where the children could not *get at* them.

get at
2 *vt insep*

find out; ascertain (see *come at* (1))
見出す，つかむ，

The truth about his sudden resignation* was difficult *to get at*.
Our object in this inquiry is *to get at* the real causes of the crash.

get at
3 *vt insep*

imply; suggest
。。。をほのめかす，言おうとする

What exactly *are* you *getting at*?
I didn't quite understand what he *was getting at* by that remark.

get at
4 *vt insep*

find fault with; criticize
。。。に文句を言う，不平を言う，当てこする

For one reason or another, the teacher seems *to be* constantly *getting at* Alex.
Who *are* you *getting at* now?

get away
vi

escape; abscond with
逃げる，。。。を持ち逃げする

The prisoner managed *to get away* (from his guards).
The thieves *got away* with a lot of cash and jewellery.
The cashier *got away* with all the money in the safe.

55

get away with
vt insep

escape punishment
。。。をうまくやり遂げる，。。。
をして無事にすむ

You really think you can *get away with* telling such obvious lies, don't you?
Some people can *get away with* murder.

get back
1 *vi*

return
帰る

When *did* you *get back* from your holiday in Spain?
I expect her *to get back* by Friday at the latest.

get back
2 *vt sep*

recover; regain
取り戻す

Sandra never *got back* the purse she lost.
If you lend him your pen, you*'ll* never *get* it *back*. I know him only too well.

get back at
vt insep

retaliate; avenge oneself
。。。に仕返しをする

He made a laughing* stock of me that night, but I*'ll get back at* him for this.
She refused to work any overtime, so the manager *got back at* her by not giving her a pay rise.

get down
1 *vt sep*

make a note of; record
記録する，書き取る

I want you *to get* his statement *down* in writing.
Have you *got* it all *down*, Mrs Briggs, or shall I repeat it for you?

get down
2 *vt sep**

depress
元気をなくさせる，滅入る

The bad news *is getting* me *down*.
You mustn't let this thing *get* you *down*. Just try to forget about it.

get down to
vt insep

apply oneself to
。。。に（真剣に）取り組む

I really must *get down to* some serious work this term.
Let's *get down to* it then, shall we?

get in 1 *vi*	arrive home 到着する，帰宅する

It was nearly midnight when they *got in*.
What time do you expect her *to get in*?

get in 2 *vi*	be elected; gain power (see *come in* (3)) 当選する，選出される

The Tories* *got in* with quite a big majority.
This political party *will* definitely *get in*, at the next general election.

get in(to) *vi, vt insep*	enter (a certain place) 。。。に入る

As all the doors and windows were shut, the dog could not *get in*.
We could not *get into* the house as it was locked and we had no key with us.

get into *vt insep*	be involved in (ある状態に) なる

They'*ll* soon *get into* debt if they are not careful with their spending.
Those boys *are* always *getting into* mischief.
I'm afraid he *got into* trouble with the police.

get off 1 *vi, vt insep*	alight (from a vehicle etc.) (馬，乗物などから) 降りる

Could you please tell me where *to get off*?
You *get off* at the next station.
You must never attempt *to get off* the bus while it is still in motion.

get off 2 *vi*	escape punishment 免れる

Next time you *won't get off* with just a warning; you'll probably end up in prison.
He was very lucky to *get off* with only a small fine*.

get on 1 *vi, vt insep*	opp. get off (1). 乗る

get on	= get along (2), (3), (4)
2 *vi*	

get on	grow old
3 *vi*	年を取る

I see he's *getting on*. Sixty next month, I believe.

get on for	approach; draw near to
vt insep	そろそろ...になる，かれこれ...に近い

Old Mrs Williams must *be getting on for* seventy.
It *was getting on for* twelve when we reached the village.

get out	leave; go
1 *vi*	...から出る，出て行く

When he refused *to get out*, she threatened to call the police.
Get out, the lot of you!

get out	leak (of a secret); become known
2 *vi*	(情報，秘密などが) 漏れる

The news *has got out* that they were secretly engaged.
Their secret is bound *to get out* sooner or later.

get out of	escape from
1 *vt insep*	...から逃げる

The rabbit *got out of* its cage because I had left the shutter open.
The convict* *has got out of* gaol by climbing a nine-foot wall.

get out of	avoid; shirk
2 *vt insep*	避ける，免れる

The boy tried *to get out of* going to school by feigning* illness.
No one should be allowed *to get out of* paying his share of the bill.
You just can't *get out of* paying your debts.

get over　　　　　　overcome; surmount
1 *vt insep*　　　　　　乗り越える，忘れる

　　　　　　　　　　　The girl used to be afraid of going to the dentist, but she *has got over* that now.
　　　　　　　　　　　He doesn't seem *to have got over* the shock of losing his wife.
　　　　　　　　　　　We have quite a lot of problems *to be got over*.

get over　　　　　　recover from
2 *vt insep*　　　　　　。。。から回復する，。。。に打ち勝つ

　　　　　　　　　　　As a little boy, Geoffrey could not *get over* the loss of his parents.
　　　　　　　　　　　It took Lisa a few weeks *to get over* her illness.

get over　　　　　　get finished with
3 *vt sep**　　　　　　やってしまう，片付ける

　　　　　　　　　　　The sooner we *get* the cleaning *over* the better.
　　　　　　　　　　　There's no point in postponing the meeting any further; we might as well *get* it *over* and done with.

get round　　　　　 cajole; wheedle
1 *vt insep*　　　　　　うまく口説く，説き伏せる

　　　　　　　　　　　The little girl *got round* her mother to buy her a new dress.
　　　　　　　　　　　I'm banking* on you, Janet, to *get round* big daddy to lend us the money.

get round　　　　　 dodge; evade; circumvent
2 *vt insep*　　　　　　うまく避ける，

　　　　　　　　　　　At the moment I see no way of *getting round* this problem.
　　　　　　　　　　　It's no use trying *to get round* paying your taxes.
　　　　　　　　　　　There're always ways and means of *getting round* the law.

get round to　　　　find time to do sth.
　vt insep　　　　　　。。。する機会をやっと見い出す

　　　　　　　　　　　I always wanted to clear out the cellar, but *have* never *got round to* it.
　　　　　　　　　　　When I finally *got round to* buying tickets for the show they were all sold out.

59

get through
1 *vt insep*

complete; finish
終る

I'm afraid I can't lend you the book now. I *haven't got through* it yet.
Will you be able *to get through* this pile of letters by tomorrow morning?

get through
2 *vi, vt insep*

pass; be successful in
合格する

The exam was quite tough, but I *got through* alright.
Did he *get through* his driving test this time?

get through
3 *vi*

make a telephone connection
電話で。。。に連絡をとる

I couldn't *get through* (to him). The line was engaged all the time.

get through
4 *vt insep*

use up; exhaust
使い果たす

He'*ll* soon *get through* his savings if he goes on spending so recklessly*.
The widow *got through* her late husband's money in just over a year.

get up
1 *vi, vt sep**

rise from bed; awaken
起きる，起こす

During the summer holidays, I used *to get up* very late.
What time *did* you *get up* this morning?
Tell the maid *to get* me *up* at seven sharp.

get up
2 *vi*

stand up
立ち上がる

The pupils *got up* when the teacher came into the classroom.
As he *was getting up* to deliver his speech, the crowd began to boo him.

get up
3 *vt sep*

organize; arrange
計画する，準備する

We're *getting up* a party for Diana's birthday, so I hope you'll all be able to come.

get up
4 *vt sep**

dress
装う，ふん装する

He *got* himself *up* as a clown for the fancy-dress* ball. The young ladies *were got up* in their best clothes.

EXERCISE 17

A Replace the underlined words with phrasal verbs containing 'get'. In some examples more than one answer is possible:

1 How is Henry progressing in his new job?
2 I wish I could finish all this work by tomorrow.
3 It took her a long time to recover from the death of her only child.
4 The teacher did not seem to be able to communicate the new material to his students.
5 The Society has organized a nation-wide campaign to raise funds for the disabled*.
6 The bank robbers escaped with fifty thousand pounds.
7 He rises from bed at six every morning.
8 This kind of thing really depresses me.
9 She can't reach the top shelf without a ladder.
10 She left her handbag in the train, but recovered it from the Lost Property Office.

B Fill in the blank spaces with the correct prepositions or particles. In some examples more than one answer is possible:

1 Unless Oliver works very hard he won't get . . . his final exams.
2 She never quite got . . . the shock of being deserted by her husband.
3 Thanks to his diligence, Gilbert got . . . of the rest of the class.
4 How are you getting . . . with your thesis?
5 Let's get the washing-up . . . before we go to the cinema.
6 A car stopped in front of the house, and a smartly dressed lady got . . . .
7 Work and worry are getting me . . . .
8 I'd better be off now; it must be getting . . . . . . ten o'clock.
9 I always wanted to paint the windows, but have never got . . . . . . it.
10 You shouldn't let him get . . . . . . a mean trick like that.

GIVE

give away
1 *vt sep*
: give free of charge
寄贈する，寄付する

He *gave away* his entire fortune to charitable foundations.
My aunt *has given* her old clothes *away* (to the poor).

give away
2 *vt sep*
: distribute; present
贈る，手渡す

A member of the royal family *gave away* the trophies.
At the end of each year the headmaster *gives away* the certificates to the students.

give away
3 *vt sep*
: betray; divulge; reveal
裏切る，漏らす，正体を暴露する

The spy said he would rather die than *give away* his country.
He said that he was not a foreigner, but his accent *gave* him *away*.

give back
vt sep
: return
返す

Having finished reading the book I *gave* it *back* (to the library).

give in
1 *vi*
: surrender; yield
降伏する，言いなりになる

The besieged* army was forced *to give in* when it ran out of ammunition*.
He says he is not going *to give in* to blackmail*, no matter what happens.

give in
2 *vt sep*
: submit; tender
提出する

Candidates who wish to take this exam should *give in* their applications not later than September 20th.
She was not satisfied with her job and decided *to give in* her notice.

give off
vt insep

emit; produce
放出する，出す

Oil refineries *give off* a lot of fumes*.
Burning rubber *gives off* an unpleasant smell.

give on to
vt insep

overlook; provide access to
．．．に面する，．．．に通じる

Their house *gives on to* the sea.
The back door *gives on to* the garden.

give out
1 *vi*

come to an end; become exhausted
使い尽くす，尽きる

Our food supplies were about *to give out* when the search party found us.
My patience is beginning *to give out*.

give out
2 *vi*

cease to function
作動しなくなる

For no apparent reason, the car engine suddenly *gave out*.

give out
3 *vt sep*

distribute
配布する

A boy standing in the street *gave out* leaflets to people passing by.
The invigilators* *gave out* the exam papers to the students.

give out
4 *vt sep*

announce; make known
アナウンスする，発表する

The newscaster *gave out* the news of the air disaster in a grave voice.
It *was given out* that the enemy had suffered heavy casualties* from the air-raid*.

give out
5 *vt insep*

= give off

63

give up 1 *vi*	despair; admit defeat （だめだと）あきらめる	

We mustn't *give up* yet; we may still find them.
I can't work out this problem; I *give up*.

give up 2 *vt insep*	stop; abandon やめる	

The old man *did not give up* horse-riding until he was sixty.
I tried *to give up* smoking, but without success.
He gave up the study of Greek long ago.

give up 3 *vt sep*	surrender; part with 自首する，譲る，手ばなす	

The fugitive* could not stand being on the run for so long and decided *to give* himself *up* (to the police).
He *gave up* his seat on the train to an elderly man.
The President refused *to give up* the documents on grounds of national security.

give up 4 *vt insep*	relinquish 断念する，やめる	

They *have given up* the idea of emigrating to Canada.
She had *to give up* her job when she got married.

give up 5 *vt sep*	devote もっぱら...に使う，ささげる	

The teachers *gave up* the last hour of their meeting to discussing the problem of truancy*.
The priest's life *was given up* to the worship of God.

EXERCISE 18

Use synonyms in place of the underlined phrasal verbs:

1 I pleaded* with him to let the boy come with us, but he refused to give in.
2 She gave back all the money she had borrowed from me.
3 Just as we were about to reach our destination the petrol gave out.
4 You must give up eating sweets if you want to get slim.

5 The news of the president's assassination was <u>given out</u> on the radio shortly before midnight.
6 This electric fire doesn't <u>give out</u> a lot of heat.
7 He <u>gave away</u> all his money to a charity.
8 Steam engines <u>give off</u> a lot of smoke.
9 One of us here must have <u>given away</u> the secret.
10 He seems determined not to <u>give up</u> his claim to the property.
11 Their villa <u>gives on</u> to the river.
12 They have <u>given up</u> all hope of finding any survivors of the air crash.
13 When did you <u>give in</u> your essay?
14 Oh, you do <u>give up</u> too easily, don't you?
15 The minister himself <u>gave away</u> the prizes.

GO

go about
1 *vi*

move from place to place
歩きまわる

These men always *go about* in gangs.

go about
2 *vi*

circulate
(うわさなどが) 広まる

A rumour *is going about* that Simon and Julie are getting engaged.
The story *is going about* that they are leaving town for good.

go about
3 *vt insep*

approach; tackle
取り組む，取りかかる

The matter is extremely delicate. We'll have *to go about* it carefully.
How do you propose *to go about* this problem?

go about with
vt insep

keep company with
。。。と付き合う

He *is going about with* a most beautiful girl.
Derek and Patricia *have been going about* (*with* each other) for some time now.

go after   pursue; try to catch
1 *vt insep*   追いかける，追跡する

The farmer *went after* the fox with a shotgun.
The police *went after* the escaped prisoner and tracked* him down a few miles from the village.

go after   try to get
2 *vt insep*   求める，追いかける

These two young men *are going after* the same girl.
He's *going after* the first prize. I know he wouldn't settle for less than that.

go against   oppose; be contrary to
1 *vt insep*   ...に反抗（反対）する，...に反する

She *went against* her parents' wishes in refusing to marry that man.
This kind of thing *goes against* my principles.

go against   be unfavourable to
2 *vt insep*   不利になる

Luck *went against* our team in the end and we lost the game.
They realized only too late that the war *was going against* them.

go ahead   proceed; continue
1 *vi*   どうぞ...してください，推進する

'May I use your telephone?' 'Please *go ahead*'.
We have decided not *to go ahead* with the project, after all.

go ahead   make progress
2 *vi*   進歩する，はかどる

The project seems *to be going ahead* well.
Once the dispute was settled, production in the plant *went ahead* full steam.

go along *vi*	proceed (with a certain activity) やっていく，進んでいく

You will learn more about the work as you *go along*.

go along with 1 *vt insep.*	accompany 同行する，ついて行く

He *went along with* his guests as far as the station.
Would you like me *to go along with* you to the doctor, or would you rather go alone?

go along with 2 *vt insep*	agree with; co-operate with 賛成する，同意する，協力する

I'm afraid I can't *go along with* you on that point.
I *go along with* you all the way.
We are quite willing *to go along with* you in this scheme.

go around *vi*	= go about (1), (2)

go at 1 *vt insep*	attack; assault 襲いかかる，攻撃する

The crazed man *went at* me with a knife.

go at 2 *vt insep*	set about energetically 取り組む

Once he decided to do the job, he *went at* it for all he was worth.

go away *vi*	go; depart; leave 行く，出掛ける

I wish you *would go away* and leave me in peace.
Are you *going away* for Christmas, or are you staying at home?

go back 1 *vi*	return 帰る，戻る

When do you intend *to go back* (to your country)?
He *went back* to the office to collect the papers he had left behind.

go back 2 *vi*	revert もとに戻る	

Let's leave this point for the moment. We'*ll go back* to it later.
But *to go back* to the problem of rising unemployment.... What's the government going to do about it?

go back 3 *vi*	date back (to) （過去に）さかのぼる	

Their family *goes back to* the Norman Conquest.
This custom *goes back to* the Elizabethan times.

go back on *vt insep*	fail to keep (one's word, promise, etc.) （約束などを）取り消す，破る	

They *have gone back on* their promise to lend us the money.
An honest man never *goes back on* his word.

go beyond *vt insep*	exceed; surpass 超える，．．．にまさる	

His account of what had happened *went beyond* credibility.
The good results *went beyond* our wildest dreams.

go by 1 *vi*	pass by （．．．のそば，前を）通る，通り過ぎる	

The parade *went by* amid*a warm applause* from the watching crowd.

go by 2 *vi*	elapse （時などが）過ぎて行く，経過する	

We were growing impatient as time *went by* and nothing happened.
As the months *went by* he got accustomed to the daily routine of prison life.

go by 3 *vt insep*	be guided by ．．．によって判断する，．．．にたよる	

One cannot always *go by* appearances, can one?
We have very little evidence *to go by*.

go down   sink
1 *vi*   沈む

The ship *went down* on her maiden voyage to Australia.
The small boat sprang a leak* and *went down* within seconds.

go down   (of the sun etc.) set
2 *vi*   没する，沈む

In the summer months the sun *goes down* very late.

go down   fall; drop
3 *vi*   下がる，減少する

The price of fruit usually *goes down* in summer.
The patient's temperature *went down* to 36.8 degrees.

go down   be received (well/badly)
4 *vi*   受け入れられる

His made-up story *went down* well with his friends.
The director's speech *went down* very badly at last night's dinner.

go for   attack
1 *vt insep*   攻撃する，襲いかかる

The dog *went for* the intruder* and chased him out of the building.
The wounded bull *went for* the matador*.

go for   go to fetch or get
2 *vt insep*   呼びに行く，取りに行く，．．．しに行く

You look very ill, Morris. Shall I *go for* the doctor?
I am *going for* a drink. Will you join me?

go for   apply to; be true of
3 *vt insep*   ．．．に当てはまる

What I have said about William *goes for* the rest of you, too.
I want everybody to leave this room, and that also *goes for* you, Barbara.

go in for 1 *vt insep*	participate in; enter for ...に参加する	

Amanda is *going in for* a beauty contest.
Are you *going in for* the 1000 metres race?

go in for 2 *vt insep*	adopt as a hobby or occupation 志す，...にたずさわる，...をする	

She *goes in for* swimming and tennis.
When he left college he *went in for* teaching.

go into *vt insep*	investigate; consider; discuss 調べる，調査する，論じる	

The detective promised that he *would go into* my case at once.
These proposals *will have to be gone into* very carefully before a final decision can be taken.
We *are* not *going into* that again, are we?

go off 1 *vi*	leave (a certain place) 去る，...へ出掛ける	

She *went off* to visit her mother abroad.
He *has gone off* to Greece for a short holiday.

go off 2 *vi*	be fired; explode 発射される，爆発する，打ち上げられる	

The gun *went off* accidentally, and wounded him in the thigh.
The boy was seriously injured when a firework *went off* in his face.

go off 3 *vi*	go bad; deteriorate 悪くなる，腐る，（質，技術が）落ちる	

The meat you bought the other day *has gone off*.
Don't eat that steak. It's *going off*.
Her work *has gone off* very much lately.

go off 4 *vi*	take place in a specified manner. (事が) 運ぶ，行なわれる	

Everything *went off* without a hitch*.
How *did* the interview *go off*?
The party *went off* very badly this time.

go off 5 *vi*	fall asleep 寝る，眠る	

He *went off* by the fire while he was watching television.

go on 1 *vi*	continue; last 続く，継続する	

I wonder how much longer this cold weather *will go on*!
It looks as though this war *will go on* forever.

go on 2 *vi*	happen; take place 起こる	

There is something fishy* *going on* in that place.
What the hell *is going on* here?

go on about *vt insep*	= keep on about	

go out 1 *vi*	leave the house (implies a leisure activity) 出掛ける	

The weather is lovely; why don't we *go out* for a walk?
They don't *go out* much these days.

go out 2 *vi*	cease to be fashionable; become obsolete すたれる，はやらなくなる	

Mini-skirts *went out* a few years ago.
This method of printing is gradually *going out*.

go out 3 *vi*	be extinguished 消える	

During the thunderstorm all the lights in the house *went out*.
The fire *went out* as I forgot to poke* it.

go over 1 *vt insep*	examine; review; inspect 調べる，検討する

The auditor* *went over* the accounts carefully.
Let's *go over* the details of the plan once more.
We *went over* the house for almost two hours and decided not to buy it.

go over 2 *vt insep*	search 入念に調べる，検査する

The customs officer *went over* my luggage, item by item.
The police officer *went over* the suspect* very thoroughly, but did not find any hidden weapons.

go round *vi, vt insep*	be sufficient (for all). (皆に) 行き渡る

Don't you worry, dear! There is enough food *to go round*.
Twenty bottles of wine *will not go round* so many guests.

go through 1 *vt insep*	= go over (1), (2)

go through 2 *vt insep*	suffer; endure; experience (苦しみを) 経験する，経る

She *has gone through* a lot with her first husband.
They *have gone through* a terrible ordeal.
The country *is going through* a critical period.

go through 3 *vt insep*	use up; consume 使い果たす，食い (飲み) 尽くす

He *has* already *gone through* the money he inherited from his uncle.
You would wonder how much food this little boy *could go through*.

go through with *vt insep*	complete; bring to a finish (仕事などを) やり通す，遂行する

I realize it is not going to be such a profitable deal, but all the same we must *go through with* it.
He says that he can't *go through with* the marriage.

go under
  vi
= go down (1)

go up
1 *vi*
increase; rise
上がる

The price of beef *has gone up* a lot since last October.
It was announced that the fees for the next academic year *would go up* by £200.

go up
2 *vi*
explode
破壊される，爆発する，（燃え）上がる

The bridge *went up* with a deafening bang.
The helicopter crashed and *went up* in flames.

go with
  vt insep
suit; match
調和する，似合う

You look ridiculous in that hat. Can't you see it *doesn't go with* your dress?
These colours *go* nicely *with* each other.

go without
  vt insep
forgo; do without
．．．なしで済ます，．．．なしで我慢する

We can't *go without* sleep for much longer.
It looks as though we shall have *to go without* a holiday this summer.
If you can't afford to buy a new suit now, you'll just have *to go without*.

EXERCISE 19

A Fill in the blank spaces with the correct prepositions or particles. In some examples more than one answer is possible:

1 He went . . . . . . this exam last year, but failed it.
2 The party went . . . until after midnight.
3 If there is not enough coffee to go . . . someone will have to go . . . .
4 Prices always seem to be going . . . . They never go . . . .
5 The bomb went . . . before the police could defuse it.
6 Do you go . . . . . . stamp-collecting?
7 I have no intention of going . . . . . . my word.
8 He wants to get a residence permit, but he does not know how to go . . . it.

9 I don't want you to help me, so please go . . . .
10 We'll soon go . . . our coal supply if we don't start economizing.

B Use synonyms in place of the underlined phrasal verbs:

1 I'll explain the new vocabulary as we <u>go along</u>.
2 The milk has <u>gone off</u> because she forgot to put it in the fridge.
3 The price of petrol will <u>go up</u> by 2p a gallon as from January.
4 He <u>went on</u> working till three in the morning.
5 Almost two years have <u>gone by</u> since we last saw him.
6 She loves to watch the sun <u>go down</u>.
7 I wonder why they <u>went off</u> in such a hurry!
8 We <u>went through</u> his papers carefully, but found nothing suspicious.
9 You <u>go back</u> now and we will come later.
10 Your brother is not very fond of work, and that <u>goes for</u> you too.
11 That yellow tie doesn't <u>go with</u> your shirt.
12 Don't <u>go by</u> what Charles says; he knows nothing about farming.
13 Bob thinks Italy will win. Do you <u>go along</u> with that?
14 The lamp in the bathroom suddenly <u>went out</u>.
15 Two fishing-boats <u>went down</u> in the storm.

HAND

hand back
vt sep

return; give back
返す

Please remember *to hand back* the cassettes you've borrowed from me. I need them for tomorrow.

hand down
vt sep

(*usu. pass.*) transmit; bequeath
伝える，残す

These customs *have been handed down* from generation to generation.
We didn't exactly buy this antique furniture. It *was handed down* to us by great-grandfather.

hand in
vt sep

submit; tender
提出する

The minister *handed in* his letter of resignation to the cabinet.
I would advise you *to hand in* your application as early as possible.

hand on *vt sep*	= hand down
hand out *vt sep*	distribute; give out 配布する，配る There was a young woman in the street, *handing out* leaflets to passers-by.
hand over *vt sep*	deliver; surrender 引き渡す，譲り渡す The Brazilian police refused *to hand over* the fugitive to the British authorities. The retiring premier* *will hand over* charge of his office on January 18th.

EXERCISE 20

Fill in the blank spaces with the correct particles:

1 As soon as I've finished marking your papers I'll hand them ... to you.
2 This legend has been handed ... from father to son.
3 Over a thousand copies of the sales brochure* have now been handed ... .
4 When the customs officer asked to see my passport I handed it ... to him.
5 She handed ... her notice yesterday and is leaving at the end of the month.

HANG

hang about 1 *vi, vt insep*	loiter (near a place) うろつく，ぶらぶらする We spent almost an hour just *hanging about*, waiting for you to come. Did you notice any suspicious-looking men *hanging about* the building at the time of the robbery?
hang about 2 *vi*	= hang on (1), hold on (1)

75

hang around = hang about (1)
vi, vt insep

hang back hesitate; show reluctance to act
vi ためらう，ちゅうちょする

He *hung back* when they asked for blood-donors*.
I suspected there was something fishy about the business, and *hung back* from taking part in it.

hang on Wait; *(see hold on (1))*
1 *vi* (少しの間) 待つ

Just *hang on* a second while I do up my dress.
Don't worry if you can't make it at seven sharp. I'*ll hang on* until eight o'clock.

hang on depend on
2 *vt insep* ．．．によって決まる，．．．しだいである

Everything *hangs on* what happens next.
His whole political career *hangs on* the result of tomorrow's election.

hang on to keep; retain possession of
vt insep しっかりと持ち続ける

I'd *hang on to* that oil painting if I were you. It might be worth a lot more in a year or two.
We must *hang on to* whatever we have.

hang together support one another
1 *vi* 団結する，一致協力する

We can overcome these difficulties if we *hang together*.
Old friends must *hang together* at all times.

hang together be consistent
2 *vi* つじつまが合う，筋道が立つ

Their statements do not seem *to hang together* at all.
His story doesn't quite *hang together*, does it?

hang up
1 *vi, vt insep*

end a telephone call abruptly
（受話器を）掛ける，（電話を）切る

She didn't give me a chance to explain; she just *hung up* (on me).

hang up
2 *vt sep*

delay; hinder
遅らす，手間取らせる，（進行を）妨げる

We *were hung up* for nearly thirty minutes during the thick fog.
I'm sorry to arrive so late, but I *got hung up* in a traffic* jam.

EXERCISE 21

Fill in the blank spaces with the correct prepositions or particles:

1 The trouble with John is that he can never hang ...... his jobs for very long.
2 Those two men have been hanging ... the place all morning. I wonder what they are up to!
3 If you'll hang ... a minute, sir, I'll go and check our files.
4 It all hangs ... now. I can see why they left in such a hurry.
5 No one hung ... when we asked for volunteers.
6 Work on the railway track has been hung ... for several weeks because of the heavy snow.
7 It all hangs ... whether he is willing to back our claim.
8 The family hung ... well during that crisis.

HOLD

hold back
1 *vt sep*

control; restrain
押える，引き止める

The police could do nothing *to hold back* the angry crowds.
She was so upset about it that she could not *hold back* her tears.

hold back
2 *vt sep*

withhold; delay
差し控える，遅らせる

This information will have *to be held back* from the witnesses until after the trial.
There will be angry protests from the transport workers if their wage increases *are held back* for much longer.

hold down
1 *vt sep*

keep at a low level
低く抑える

The government came in for sharp criticism from the Opposition* leader for failing *to hold down* prices.
Unless our expenditure* *is held down*, we'll soon go bankrupt*.

hold down
2 *vt sep*

suppress; oppress
抑えつける，抑圧する

The country *is* being ruthlessly* *held down* by the occupying armies.

hold forth
vi

harangue; make a speech
述べ立てる，ながながとしゃべる

He *held forth* at great length on the evils of the permissive* society.

hold in
vt sep

suppress; restrain
抑制する，自制する，控える

You must learn *to hold in* your bad temper.
She's used to *holding in* her feelings.

hold off
1 *vi*

(of rain etc.) stay away
（雨などが）降ろうとしない

I hope the rain will *hold off* until after the match.

hold off
2 *vt sep*

keep at a distance
寄せつけない，（敵の攻撃を）阻止する

The besieged garrison* *held off* enemy attacks for several days.

hold on 1 *vi*	wait (see *hang on* (1)) 待つ
	If you *hold on* a moment, madam, I'll go and see if Mr Jones is free. Just *hold on* a second while I put my shoes on.
hold on 2 *vi*	see *hold out* (2)
hold on to *vt insep*	keep in one's hands or possession しっかりしがみつく，手放さないでいる
	He mananged *to hold on to* the rope until he was rescued. He wanted to sell that piece of land, but I persuaded him *to hold on to* it.
hold out 1 *vi*	last; continue 続く，（蓄えなどが）持つ
	Our food supplies won't *hold out* for much longer. How long *will* these provisions* *hold out*?
hold out 2 *vi*	continue to resist 持ちこたえる，抵抗する
	The small force *held out* heroically against overwhelming odds. The beleaguered* town *held out* for four weeks till reinforcements* arrived.
hold over *vt sep**	(*usu. pass.*) postpone; defer 持ち越す，延ばす
	The last item on the agenda* *will be held over* until the next meeting. The decision to close down the factory *has been held over* until April.
hold to *vt insep*	adhere to 固守する
	I think we ought to *hold to* our original plan. He *has* never *held to* his principles very firmly.

hold together *vi, vt sep*	remain or keep united 団結を続ける	

We can only hope that the country *will hold together* during this crisis.
If he can't *hold* the Party *together*, no one can.

hold up 1 *vt sep*	delay; hinder 遅らせる，妨げる	

We *were held up* in a traffic jam for nearly one hour.
Mail delivery *has been held up* for a few days as a result of the post office workers' strike.

hold up 2 *vt sep*	stop with intent to rob 襲う，．．．から強奪する	

The police are reported to be looking for three men who *held up* a mail van in East London this morning.
Two armed men *held up* the bank in broad daylight.

hold with *vt insep*	approve of; agree with 賛成する，同意する，．．．を可とする	

They don't *hold with* Communism and all that it stands for.
Do you *hold with* smoking in cinemas?

EXERCISE 22

Fill in the blank spaces with the correct prepositions or particles:

1 I simply couldn't hold ... my anger. The whole thing was outrageous*.
2 The Catholic Church does not hold ... divorce.
3 The train was held ... by fog for almost two hours.
4 Lazy, restless people can't hold ...... their jobs.
5 Hold ... a minute! Can't you see I'm busy?
6 I don't hold ... all this talk about women's lib and sex equality.
7 They were held ... at gun point by three masked men.
8 The garrison held ... for two weeks before surrendering.
9 Does he still hold ... what he said last time?
10 The family has always held ... in difficult times like these.
11 If you want me to help you, then don't try to hold the truth ... from me.
12 We have been held ... by this dictator long enough; it's time we got rid of him.

KEEP

keep at
vt insep

persist in; persevere in
根気よく...をする，熱心に...をする

Arthur *kept at* his German until it was perfect.
You will never finish the job unless you *keep at* it.

keep away
vi, vt sep*

(cause to) stay away
...に近寄らない，近付けない

He *kept away* from his friends for several months.
You'd better *keep away* from that girl, or you'll get yourself into trouble.
Keep the child *away* from that fire.

keep back
1 *vi, vt sep*

(cause to) stay back
...から後ろにさがる，...に近寄らない

The firemen asked the crowd *to keep back* from the burning building.
Keep back, or I'll shoot!
The policemen could do nothing *to keep* the jubilant* fans *back* from the pitch.

keep back
2 *vt sep*

conceal; keep secret
(秘密などを）隠す

We were certain she *was keeping* something *back* from us, but we didn't know exactly what.
For the time being, all the names of the witnesses will have *to be kept back*.

keep back
3 *vt sep*

hinder; impede; delay
邪魔する，妨げる

What *has kept* you *back* for so long?
I hope I'm not *keeping* you *back* from your work.

keep down
1 *vt sep**

repress; hold in subjection
仰える，仰えつける

The conquered peoples *were kept down* by cruel, restrictive laws.

keep down 2 *vt sep*	keep low 低く抑える	

The government seems unable *to keep down* prices. They are going up all the time.
Ask those two men *to keep* their voices *down*. I can hardly hear a word of what the speaker is saying.

keep from *vt insep*	avoid; refrain from 。。。せずにいる，慎しむ，避ける	

You should *keep from* making promises you know you can't fulfil.
Though his health was rapidly deteriorating, he could not *keep from* alcohol.

keep in 1 *vt sep*	detain after school hours as a punishment （罰として放課後）残す	

The schoolmaster *kept in* all the pupils who had not done their homework.

keep in 2 *vt sep*	restrain; suppress 抑える，隠す	

She is very good at *keeping in* her emotions.
The speaker managed *to keep* his indignation* *in*, in spite of the provocative* remarks from the audience.

keep in with *vt insep*	remain friendly with 。。。と調子よくやる，仲よくする	

You should *keep in with* your boss if you expect any further promotion.
When she won a fortune on the pools all her friends and relatives tried *to keep in with* her.

keep off 1 *vi*	(of rain, etc.) stay away （雨が）降り出さない	

Fortunately, the rain *kept off* the whole afternoon and we were able to finish our game.

keep off 2 *vi, vt sep*	(cause to) stay at a distance from 近づけない，入らない
	'*Keep off* the grass!' (sign displayed in public parks). This barbed wire is meant *to keep* trespassers* *off*.
keep on *vi*	(followed by gerund) continue 。。。し続ける
	Don't *keep on* telling me what to do; I'm perfectly capable of making my own decisions. Why do you have *to keep on* bothering me?
keep on about *vt insep*	keep talking about (sb. or sth.) (see *go on about*) （うるさいほど）しゃべり続ける
	The way she *keeps on about* her son! It's enough to bore anyone to tears. I wish that woman wouldn't *keep on about* her arthritis*; I'm sick and tired of listening to her.
keep on at *vt insep*	pester with requests, etc. 。。。にうるさく言う
	He won't give you back your money unless you *keep on at* him all the time.
keep out *vi, vt sep*	(cause to) stay outside 中に入らない，入れない，締め出す
	'Private. *Keep out*!' (notice on door) Tell those kids *to keep out* of my study, please! These old windows *do* not *keep out* the draught*. You really mustn't *keep* the cat *out* in this cold weather.
keep out of *vt insep*	not interfere in 。。。に関係しない
	Now you *keep out of* this! It's no concern of yours. I'd *keep out of* their quarrel if I were you.
keep to *vt insep*	adhere to 固く守る
	He's not the kind of person who *keeps to* his promises. Please make sure that this schedule *is* strictly *kept to*.

keep up
1 *vt sep*

maintain; continue
続ける

You are doing just fine, Sally. *Keep* it *up*!
They had *kept up* a steady correspondence for nearly eight years.
We should try *to keep up* these old customs of our ancestors.

keep up
2 *vt sep*

maintain in good condition
維持する，良好な（行き届いた）状態にしておく

We can no longer afford *to keep up* this big house, so we may have to sell it and buy a smaller one.

keep up
3 *vt sep**

delay from going to bed
(寝かさずに) 起こしておく

The baby was sick last night and *kept* us *up* until the small hours.
We'd better be off now; we don't want *to keep* you *up*.

keep up with
vt insep

keep pace with
(人，時勢などに) 遅れない

Can Russia *keep up with* America in the field of space technology?
Eva has to work very hard in order to *keep up with* her classmates.

EXERCISE 23

Fill in the blank spaces with the correct prepositions or particles:

1 They are finding it difficult to keep ... such a large house.
2 Tell that man to keep his cattle ... my land.
3 She keeps ...... her ailments* for hours on end.
4 Don't walk so fast; I can't keep ...... you.
5 Her mother kept her ... from school yesterday to help her with some housework.
6 Don't keep ... interrupting him; let him finish what he has to say.
7 She kept ...... her husband until he agreed to buy her a new washing-machine.
8 They kept the bad news ... from her for as long as they could.
9 This new anorak I've bought you should keep ... the cold.

10 You will soon finish this work if you keep ... it for a few more days.
11 We have been kept ... in our training programme by shortage of qualified staff.
12 The shopkeeper has kept ... his reputation by selling first-class goods.
13 You should keep ... doing anything that might antagonize* him.
14 The teacher kept Elizabeth ... yesterday for being late.
15 The rebellious* tribes could only be kept ... by cruel measures.

KNOCK

knock about
1 *vt insep*

wander here and there
。。。のあちこちを歩きまわる

Our son *has knocked about* the world a great deal.
He *has been knocking about* Africa ever since he left the army.

knock about
2 *vt sep**

treat roughly; maltreat
（人や物を）乱暴に扱う

It's wrong *to knock* your children *about* in this way.
The furniture *has been* badly *knocked about*.

knock back
1 *vt sep*

drink at one gulp
ぐっと飲む

He ordered a pint of beer and *knocked* it *back* in ten seconds.
She *knocked back* two double brandies.

knock back
2 *vt sep**

= set back (3)

knock down
1 *vt sep*

strike to the ground
打ち倒す，なぐり倒す，（車が）はねる

The boxer *knocked down* his opponent with a single punch.
The old man *was knocked down* by a lorry as he was crossing the street.

knock down 2 *vt sep*	demolish; pull down 取り壊す	

Quite a lot of old houses in this area *have been knocked down* and replaced by modern blocks of flats.

knock down 3 *vt sep*	sell at an auction 競り落す	

The auctioneer *knocked* the painting *down* to an art dealer from Paris.
That beautiful mahogany desk *was knocked down* to me for only a fiver.

knock down 4 *vt sep*	reduce (a price, etc.) 下げる，安くする	

The shopkeeper *knocked* the price *down* from £10 to £8.

knock off 1 *vi*	stop work やめる	

We usually *knock off* at about five o'clock.
What time do you *knock off* for lunch?

knock off 2 *vt sep*	cause to fall 打ち落す	

You'd better keep an eye on the child, or he'*ll knock* that vase *off*.
The unfortunate jockey was knocked off his horse and broke his arm.

knock off 3 *vt sep*	compose hurriedly 手早く仕上げる，さっさとやってしまう	

I'm not surprised he got a low mark for his essay. He *knocked* it *off* in less than an hour.
She *knocked off* an article for a magazine in about two hours.

knock off 4 *vt sep*	deduct 割り引く，差し引く	

I'*ll knock off* 40p if you want to buy the book.
The shopkeeper *knocked* four pounds *off* the bill.

knock out
1 *vt sep*

render unconscious
ノックアウトする，へとへとにする

The boxing champion *knocked* his challenger *out* in the fourth round of the fight.
It only took three glasses of wine *to knock* him *out* for the rest of the evening.

knock out
2 *vt sep*

eliminate from a competition
（競技で相手を）敗退させる

Italy *knocked* England *out* (of the World Cup), and *were* themselves *knocked out* by Holland.

knock up
1 *vt sep*

rouse; awaken
呼び起こす

Tell the maid *to knock* me *up* at eight sharp.
People don't like being *knocked up* in the middle of the night.

knock up
2 *vt sep*

prepare quickly
大急ぎで作る．(用意する)

She *knocked up* a meal for her unexpected guests.
I don't have time to cook a proper lunch, so I'*ll* just *knock up* a snack for us.

knock up
3 *vt sep**

exhaust
疲れきる

I don't want you *to knock* yourself *up* like that.
What's the matter, Jim? You look quite *knocked up*.

EXERCISE 24

Fill in the blank spaces with the correct prepositions or particles:

1. The workmen usually knock ... for tea at three o'clock.
2. Her husband knocks her ... a bit, but she has learnt to put up with it.
3. Our team was knocked ... of the competition earlier than expected.
4. They have knocked that old house ... and built a new one in its place.
5. He has been knocking ... Scandinavia for some time, but he is now back home.
6. She was knocked ... by a taxi and had to be taken to hospital.

87

7. The salesman agreed to knock five pounds ... the price of the radio.
8. I was completely knocked ... after that long journey.
9. The boxer regained his title by knocking his opponent* ....
10. I have to get up early tomorrow, so could you please knock me ... at six?

LAY

lay aside
1 *vt sep*

place to one side
(一時) わきへ置く

He *laid aside* his book and listened to what I had to tell him.

lay aside
2 *vt sep*

abandon; disregard
捨てる，やめる，放棄する

At such a time of crisis, party differences should be *laid aside*.

lay aside
3 *vt sep*

save for the future (see *put aside/away/by*)
取っておく，貯える

You should look ahead and try *to lay aside* some money for your retirement.
We have a few hundred pounds *laid aside* for emergencies.

lay down
1 *vt sep*

place down
下に置く，降ろす

They *laid down* the heavy box gently.
The soldiers *laid down* their arms (i.e. surrendered).
She *laid* the baby *down* on the bed.

lay down
2 *vt sep*

impose; prescribe
規定する，主張する

The bank *has laid down* certain conditions on which the loan may be granted.
He is that type of person who likes *to lay down* the law.
The rules of procedure in a conference *are laid down* to deal with any point of order.

lay down 3 *vt insep*	(with 'life') sacrifice (。。。のために命を）ささげる，捨てる

A man who *lays down* his life for his country is certainly worthy of praise.
This was a cause which they believed was just, and for which they were prepared *to lay down* their lives.

lay in *vt sep*	store 貯える，買い込む

Make sure you *lay in* plenty of food and drink for the week-end.
We *laid in* a large supply of sugar before it went up in price.

lay off 1 *vt sep*	dismiss temporarily 一時解雇する

The factory *has laid off* some two hundred workers during the last three months.
More and more people *are being laid off* every day as a result of the present economic depression*.

lay off 2 *vt insep*	desist from (不快，有害なことを）やめる

If only you'd *lay off* smoking for a while, I'm sure you'd feel much better.
Lay off teasing that cat, Janet!

lay on 1 *vt sep*	supply; provide (ガス，水道，電気などを）引く

How long will it take *to lay on* water in this house?
We'll move into our new cottage as soon as gas and electricity *have been laid on*.

lay on 2 *vt sep*	arrange; organize 計画を立てる

They *have laid on* a splendid concert for their distinguished visitors.
We *are laying on* a party for Joanna's birthday.

lay on 3 *vt sep*	apply; spread （ペンキ，ニスなどを）塗る	

There is still one more coat of paint *to be laid on*.

lay out 1 *vt sep*	spend; disburse （金を）出す，使う，投資する	

We had *to lay out* every penny we had saved on that house.
I *have* already *laid out* an awful lot of money on repairs to this car.

lay out 2 *vt sep*	make unconscious 気絶させる，打ち倒す	

He received a blow on his chin, which *laid* him *out*.
The heat of the sun *laid* her *out*.

lay out 3 *vt sep*	plan; arrange 計画する，配置計画する，レイアウトする	

The gardener *laid out* the flower-beds very neatly.
The printer *lays out* the pages of a book.

lay out 4 *vt sep*	prepare for burial 埋葬の準備をする	

The undertaker* carefully *laid out* the corpse*.
The corpse *is* now *laid out* and ready for burial.

lay up 1 *vt sep*	store; stock 蓄える	

'*Lay* not *up* for yourselves treasures upon earth, where moth* and rust doth*corrupt*, and where thieves break through and steal: but *lay up* for yourselves treasures in heaven.' – The Bible

lay up 2 *vt sep*	take out of service （車を車庫に）しまい込む	

I've had *to lay up* my car; I simply can't afford the petrol.
These ships *have been laid up* for repairs.

lay up
3 *vt sep*

(*usu. pass.*) confine to bed
(病気，けがが）人を働けなくする，
引きこもらせる

A really bad attack of 'flu can *lay* you *up* for days.
He *was laid up* for two months with a broken leg.

EXERCISE 25

Use synonyms in place of the underlined phrasal verbs:
1. Owing to the drop in sales, the factory is laying some of the men off.
2. You should try to lay your prejudices* aside and judge the case on its merits.
3. The grounds of the mansion were laid out by a landscape architect.
4. I wish you would lay off drink for a little while!
5. Electricity will be laid on in the house within the next few days.
6. She has been laid up with malaria for the last two weeks.
7. The government is laying out large sums of money on its development programmes.
8. He usually lays up his car during the winter months.
9. You just can't lay down hard and fast rules.
10. They laid up large supplies of coal for the severe winter ahead.
11. We have a nice little sum of money laid aside for a rainy day.
12. She laid in a good stock of rice in case of a shortage.

LEAVE

leave aside
vt sep

disregard; not consider
無視する，軽視する，放置する

I don't quite see how you can *leave aside* the fact that the man is a crook*.
Let us *leave* this matter *aside* for the moment, shall we?

leave behind
1 *vt sep*

fail to bring; forget to take
置き去りにする，置き忘れる

Next time you come to see us, remember not *to leave* Marilyn *behind*.
She *left* her luggage *behind* in the train.
I can't give you a lift today, as I have *left* the car *behind*.

leave behind
2 *vt sep*

outstrip
追い越す，．．．にまさる

Towards the end of the race, Alan was rapidly *leaving* the other runners *behind*.
In mathematics, she *leaves* everyone else way *behind*.

leave off
1 *vi, vt insep*

stop; cease
(雨が) やむ，やめる

It started to rain at six in the evening, and never *left off* all night.
Last time, we *left off* at the end of Lesson Four.
Leave off arguing you two, and get on with the job.

leave off
2 *vt sep*

cease to wear
服の着用をやめる，脱ぐ

Now that the winter months are over, we can *leave off* our woolen garments*.
In this cold climate, winter clothing cannot usually *be left off* before May.

leave on
1 *vt sep*

allow to stay in position
(かぶった，着た，掛けた) ままにしておく

He *left on* his hat when he went into the house.
Don't remove that cover; *leave* it *on*.

leave on
2 *vt sep*

not switch off
点けたままにしておく

Don't *leave* the television *on* when you are not watching it.
The light in the bathroom *had been left on* all night.

leave out
1 *vt sep**

leave outside
外に出したままにしておく

He went in and *left* the others *out* in the rain.
If you *leave* your toys *out* at night, darling, someone might steal them.

leave out
2 *vt sep*

omit; skip
省く，抜かす，落とす

Before we can print this book, you will have *to leave out* all the four-letter words.
It would be a great pity *to leave* this material *out*.
You *left out* one crucial point, didn't you?

leave out
3 *vt sep*

exclude (from)
忘れる，抜かす，除外する

Make sure you don't *leave out* anyone from the invitations.
He *has been left out* of the team, after all.

leave over
1 *vt sep**

postpone; defer
延期する

This matter will have *to be left over* until we meet again in April.

be left over
2 *vt sep*

remain
残る，余る

When they had finished eating, there *was* hardly any food *left over*.

EXERCISE 26

Fill in the blank spaces with the correct particles:

1 Tell that girl to leave ... crying, will you?
2 He left his coat ... in the office, and had to go back for it.
3 She took up the tale at the point where she had left ....
4 You can leave that light ... ; I'll switch it off when I go to bed.
5 The last item on the agenda will be left ... until our next meeting.
6 We left ... our sweaters when the weather got warm.
7 The editor could not publish my article in its entirety, so I had to leave parts of it ....
8 Please don't leave me ... ; I want to come with you.
9 We normally leave ... work at about five every day.
10 Let us leave that question ... now and concentrate on this one.

LET

let down　　　　lower
1 *vt sep*　　　　降ろす，（髪を）解く

He *let down* the rope to the men below.
When she *lets* her hair *down* it almost reaches her waist.

let down　　　　lengthen (a garment)
2 *vt sep*　　　　（衣服の丈を）延ばす

Your dress is too short and needs *to be let down* several inches.

let down　　　　fail; disappoint
3 *vt sep*　　　　。。。の期待を裏切る，がっかりさせる

He never *lets down* anyone who turns to him for help.
I'll do everything I can to help you. I won't *let* you *down*.

let in　　　　allow to enter
　vt sep　　　　入れる，通す，漏る

She opened the door and *let* the cat *in*.
These old leather boots *let in* a lot of water.
Don't *let* any strangers *in* while we are out.

let in for　　　　involve sb. in
　*vt sep**　　　　（損失，困難などに）陥れる，巻き込ませる

You realize what you have *let* yourself *in for* by signing those papers, don't you?
He has *let* us *in for* a lot of extra work by failing to turn up.

let off　　　　excuse; punish lightly
1 *vt sep*　　　　放免する，（軽い罰で）許す

I'll *let* you *off* this time if you promise never to do it again.
The magistrate* *let off* the petty* thief with a small fine.

let off 2 *vt sep*	explode; discharge 撃つ，放つ，打ち上げる

In England it is traditional that children *let off* fireworks on November 5th.
He *let* the gun *off* accidentally and wounded himself in the thigh.

let on *vi*	tell (esp. sth. secret) 告げ口する，（秘密を）漏らす

She knew who the culprit* was, but she did not *let on*.
Don't *let on* that I've given you a pay rise. I don't want the others to know about it.

let out 1 *vt sep*	allow to go out 外に出す，（空気などを）抜く

Open the gate and *let out* the cattle!
Some boys *let* the air *out* of the front tyres of my car.

let out 2 *vt sep*	disclose; divulge （うっかり）口外する，漏らす

Please keep this information to yourself. Don't *let* it *out* to anyone else.
I should like to know who *let out* the secret.

let out 3 *vt sep*	make looser (a garment) （衣服を）広げる，ゆるめる，伸ばす

The dress is not a bad fit, but it needs *letting out* a little round the waist.

let out 4 *vt insep*	utter （声，うめき声などを）あげる

The injured man *let out* a cry of pain.
She *let out* a loud scream which was heard in the whole building.

let up 1 *vi*	abate; stop やむ，静まる

The storm raged all day, showing no signs of *letting up*.
'Has the rain *let up* yet?' 'No, it's still pouring down'.

let up
2 *vi*

slacken one's efforts
努力をゆるめる，手を休める，くつろぐ

We can't afford *to let up*, now that we've nearly accomplished* our task.
He worked at it all day; he never *let up* for a moment.

EXERCISE 27

Fill in the blank spaces with the correct particles:

1 Caroline has put on so much weight that she has had to let ... all her clothes.
2 We mustn't let ... about where they are hiding.
3 He was very lucky to be let ... with a warning and no other punishment.
4 If the pain doesn't let ... and he can't sleep, give him a sedative.*
5 Miraculously, no one was hurt when a bomb was let ... inside the shopping centre.
6 The news must have been let ... to the Press by some officials in this department.
7 I thought I could rely on your discretion,* but you let me ....
8 You are letting yourself ...... a lot of unnecessary trouble.
9 To lengthen a skirt is to let it ....
10 The door-keeper won't let ... anyone who hasn't got a membership card.

LOOK

look after
 vt insep

take care of
。。。の世話をする

The nurse *looks after* the children when we go away.
I'm perfectly capable of *looking after* myself.
She obviously knows how *to look after* her body.

look at
1 *vt insep*

gaze at
見る，見つめる

She stood *looking at* the painting in admiration.
The two men *looked* uneasily *at* each other.
To look at him you'd never think he was a professor.

look at   examine; inspect
2 *vt insep*   考察する，調べる

          The doctor *looked at* my knee and said there was nothing wrong with it.
          We must *look at* the question from all sides.

look at   view; see
3 *vt insep*   見る，。。。の見方をする

          Being not so young, she *looks at* life differently from you and me.
          Everyone has his own way of *looking at* things.

look at   (*usu. neg.*) consider
4 *vt insep*   考える，相手にする

          He wouldn't even *look at* my offer.
          They refuse *to look at* our proposals.

look away   turn the eyes in another direction
   vi   目をそらす

          When he entered the room the girl was partially undressed, and they both *looked away* in embarrassment.

look back   look behind
1 *vi*   後ろを見る，振り返る

          Don't *look back* now, but I think we are being followed.

look back   reflect upon the past
2 *vi*   回顧する，振り返って見る

          Looking back, I suppose we are no better off than we were twenty-five years ago.
          People like *to look back* on the good old days.

look down   look downwards
   vi   見おろす，うつむく

          He leaned over the window-sill* and *looked down* at the trees below.
          The little girl *looked down* shyly and would not speak to anyone.

look down on　　despise; regard with contempt
vt insep　　。。。を見おろす，軽べつする

　　One should never *look down on* people merely because they are poor.
　　These days unskilled workers are *looked down on* by everyone.

look for　　search for; seek
1 *vt insep*　　捜す，探す

　　She *is looking for* a job as a shorthand* typist.
　　We *are looking for* a young man with drive* and initiative to fill this vacancy.
　　What *are* you *looking for*?

look for　　expect
2 *vt insep*　　期待する

　　I warned you not to get involved with that fellow, so don't *look for* any help from me now.
　　What do you *look for* in a woman?

look forward to　　anticipate with pleasure
vt insep　　楽しみにして待つ

　　We *are looking forward to* meeting your wife.
　　I *am looking forward to* the Christmas holidays.

look in　　pay a short visit (to)
vi　　立ち寄る，ちょっと訪ねる

　　The doctor *will look in* again this evening to see if everything is all right.
　　Look in on me next time you are in London, won't you?

look into　　investigate; examine
vt insep　　調査する，調べる

　　The police said that they *would look into* the matter at once.
　　Your complaint is being carefully *looked into*.

98

look on 1 *vi*	be a spectator 傍観する，見物する
	They stood *looking on* while he was being attacked. I don't want to take part in this game; I'd rather *look on*.
look on 2 *vt insep*	consider; regard 。。。とみなす，。。。と考える
	Some people *look on* him as a hero; others as a traitor*. He *is looked (up)on* as the greatest novelist of his time.
look on to *vt insep*	overlook; face 。。。に面する，。。。に向いている
	Their house *looks on to* Hyde Park. My bedroom *looks on to* the river.
look out 1 *vi*	look outwards 外を見る
	She stood at the window and *looked out* at the hills.
look out 2 *vi*	(*usu. imper.*) take care! beware! 気をつけよ！　注意しなさい！
	Look out! The road is icy *Look out*! You nearly ran over that child.
look out for 1 *vt insep*	watch for 見つける，。。。に気をつける
	Look out for me at the station. I'll be at the information desk. When you walk through that field you must *look out for* snakes.
look out for 2 *vt insep*	search carefully for 捜す，探す
	We've been *looking out for* a new house for the last two months, but haven't found anything suitable yet.
look out on *vt insep*	= look on to

99

look over
vt sep

inspect; examine.
。。。に目を通す，。。。を（ざっと）調べる

We ought to get a surveyor* *to look over* the house before we decide to buy it.
I'd like you *to look* the contract *over* for me if you can spare the time.
Look over your essay before you hand it in.

look round
1 *vi*

= look back (1)

look round
2 *vi, vt insep*

tour; visit (a place)
あちこち見てまわる，視察する

We did not have much time *to look round* (the city).
A party of foreign visitors *were looking round* the factory this morning.

look through
1 *vt insep*

direct the eyes through
。。。を通して見る

She *looked through* the window at the snow-covered hills.
He *looked through* his binoculars* to get a clearer view of the castle.

look through
2 *vt insep*

examine; study; peruse
一通り調べる，ざっと見る

Look through these photographs and see if you can pick her out.
He always *looks through* the morning papers before breakfast.
We *have looked through* our files, but found no one by the name of Bloggs.

look to
1 *vt insep*

attend to; take care of
。。。に注意する，気をつける

Every citizen must *look to* his duties.
Look to it that this doesn't happen again.

look to
2 *vt insep*

turn to; rely on
当てにする，頼りにする

He is hardly the right person *to look to* for advice.
'You can always *look to* me for help', said the father to his son.

look up
1 *vi*

look upwards
見上げる，目を上げる

He lay down on the bed and *looked up* at the ceiling.
She didn't even *look up* from her book when I came into the room.

look up
2 *vi*

improve
上向きになる，よくなる

If they can afford a new house things must be *looking up* for them.
Thank goodness the weather *is looking up*.

look up
3 *vt sep*

visit (a person)
訪問する，立ち寄る

When you go to Italy, Frank, I'd like you *to look up* an old friend in Rome.
She always *looks* me *up* when she is in town.

look up
4 *vt sep*

search for; try to find
調べる

You can *look up* the difficult words in your dictionary.
Would you be kind enough *to look up* the time of the next bus to Leeds for me?

look up and down
 vt sep*

look at (sb.) contemptuously
じろじろ見る，軽べつしたように見る

The sergeant *looked* the soldier *up and down* and ordered him to button his uniform.

look up to
 vt insep

admire; regard with esteem
。。。を見上げる，尊敬する，賞賛する

She *looks up to* people with plenty of money.
Teenagers usually *look up to* pop* stars.

EXERCISE 28

A Use synonyms in place of the underlined phrasal verbs:

1. We must get a plumber to look at those pipes.
2. Business has been rather slack lately, but now it seems to be looking up.
3. I've looked for my lighter everywhere, but I still can't find it.
4. They wouldn't even look at my suggestion.
5. Will you look after the baby while I go shopping?
6. Two boys were having a fight while their friends were looking on.
7. Do look me up if ever you come to Oxford.
8. We are looking into the possibility of offering you a permanent contract with our firm.
9. Look through the agreement before you sign it.
10. I've always looked on you as one of my best friends.

B Fill in the blank spaces with the correct prepositions or particles:

1. Look . . . on your way home. I have something important to tell you.
2. If you go swimming there you must look . . . . . . sharks.
3. The police are looking . . . three men who broke out of gaol yesterday.
4. If you don't have her number with you look it . . . in the telephone directory.
5. We are looking . . . . . . seeing you again, Geoffrey.
6. Look . . . ! There is a car coming.
7. When I passed her in the street she just looked . . . pretending not to see me.
8. The old actress looked . . . wistfully* on her youth.
9. She heard a noise behind her and looked . . . to see what it was.
10. They are very snobbish and look . . . . . . the working-class.

MAKE

make after *vt insep*	pursue; chase 追う，追跡する

The policeman *made after* the thief.
The dogs *made after* the rabbit at an incredible speed.

make at *vt insep*	attack; lunge at 。。。に向って進む，襲いかかる

The man *made at* me with a big knife.

make away with
vt insep

kill; murder
殺す

He *made away with* his wife by poisoning her food.
She threatened *to make away with* herself if he ever left her.

make for
1 *vt insep*

go towards; head for
。。。の方向へ進む，。。。に近づく

The ship *was making for* Dover.
Where *are* you *making for*?

make for
2 *vt insep*

lead to; result in
（ある結果と）なる

Money does not always *make for* happiness.
Hygienic* kitchens *make for* healthy homes.

make off
vi

escape; run away
急いで去る，逃亡する

As soon as they saw the policeman coming, the thieves *made off*.

make off with
vt insep

decamp with
持ち逃げする

The robbers *made off with* a lot of cash and jewellery.
Some boys *have made off with* our luggage.

make out
1 *vt sep*

write; complete
作成する，書く

He *made out* a cheque for two hundred pounds.
Make out a list of the things you need at the grocer's.
Applications for this post should be *made out* in duplicate.

make out
2 *vt sep*

pretend; claim; maintain
見せかける，ふりをする，。。。のように言う

She *makes* herself *out* to be wealthier than she really is.
He *made out* that he had no previous knowledge of the deal.
He is not so bad as he *is made out* to be.

make out 3 *vt sep*	understand 理解する	

He is a strange sort of fellow. I cannot *make* him *out* at all.
I can't *make out* why she hasn't told me about it before.

make out 4 *vt sep*	distinguish; discern 見分ける，識別する	

I couldn't *make out* his face; it was too dark.
We could just *make* the castle *out* in the distance.

make out 5 *vt sep*	decipher 判読する	

Can you *make out* the postmark on this letter?
See if you can *make out* this signature.

make over *vt sep*	transfer the ownership of sth. 譲渡する	

He *has made over* his estate to his niece.
The bulk of the property *was made over* to the eldest son.

make up 1 *vi, vt sep*	apply cosmetics to the face 化粧する，メーキャップする	

A young girl like you shouldn't need *to make up*.
It takes my wife ages *to make up* her face.
He doesn't like women who *are* heavily *made up*.

make up 2 *vt sep*	invent; fabricate (話などを) でっち上げる，作り出す	

I'm not very good at *making up* excuses, I'm afraid.
Now admit it; you *made* that story *up*, didn't you?
I wish you would stop *making* things *up*, Janice!

make up
3 *vt sep*

compensate for, recoup
補う，埋め合わせる，取り返す

We expect the government *to make up* our loss in profits this year.
There is a lot of leeway* *to make up* if you want to have a chance of passing your exams.

make up
4 *vt sep*

complete; supplement
（補って全体，必要数を）満たす，完全にする

How much do you need *to make up* the total?
We still need a hundred pounds *to make up* the deficit.

make up
5 *vt insep*

compose; constitute; form
構成する

Thirty-three different countries *make up* the British Commonwealth.
The human body *is made up* of millions of cells.

make up
6 *vt sep*

compound; put together
調合する，取りまとめる

The chemist *made up* the doctor's prescription*.
She *made up* a bundle of old clothes and sent it off to a charity.

make up
7 *vt sep*

tailor; sew
仕立てる

If you take this suit length to the tailor, he'll *make it up* for you.
'Customers' own materials *made up*'. (notice outside tailor's shop)

make up
8 *vi, vt sep*

become reconciled; settle (a quarrel)
仲直りする

After their quarrel they kissed and *made up*.
It's time you *made up* that silly quarrel.
Have Paul and Jean *made it up* yet?
Has Paul *made it up* with Jean yet?

make up 9 *vt sep*	(with 'mind') come to a decision 決心する	

Have you *made up* your mind yet?
You have a whole week in which *to make up* your mind.
My mind *is made up*. I am not going on that trip.

make up for *vt insep*	compensate for 埋め合わせる，補う	

You must work very hard now *to make up for* all the time you have wasted.
You had better *make up for* the damage you have caused.

make up to *vt insep*	ingratiate oneself with （目上の人などに）取り入る，へつらう	

The new secretary has already started *making up to* the boss.
He is tired of being constantly *made up to* by his juniors.

EXERCISE 29

Replace the underlined words with phrasal verbs containing *make*:

1 The audience largely <u>consisted</u> of very young men and women. (*use the passive*)
2 There was so much noise that I could not <u>understand</u> what the speaker was saying.
3 I don't believe a word of what he said. I think he <u>invented</u> it all.
4 The dictator has <u>killed</u> most of his opponents.
5 His handwriting is very difficult to <u>decipher</u>.*
6 The bandits <u>pursued</u> us on horseback.
7 We could just <u>discern</u>* the ship on the horizon.
8 As soon as they finished work they <u>headed for</u> the local pub.
9 I haven't much money on me. Do you mind if I <u>write</u> you a cheque?
10 A year before he died grandfather <u>transferred</u> the business to me.
11 The boys <u>ran away</u> when they caught sight of me.
12 He is not so stupid as some people <u>maintain</u>.
13 Unlike children, adults don't <u>settle</u> their quarrels quickly.
14 The cashier has <u>decamped</u>*with almost five hundred pounds.
15 I hope this cheque will <u>compensate for</u> all the trouble you have gone through.
16 Good working conditions <u>lead to</u> increased productivity.

PASS

pass away
1 *vi*

die
死ぬ

The old man *passed away* peacefully in his sleep.
I'm sorry to hear that your father *has passed away*.

pass away
2 *vi*

disappear; vanish
消え去る，過ぎ去る

The old cultural values seem to have *passed away*.
Let us hope our difficulties *will* soon *pass away*.

pass by
1 *vi, vt insep*

go past
通り過ぎる

I saw her *passing by* only a short while ago.
The procession *passed by* our house.

pass by
2 *vt sep**

ignore, overlook
無視する

He had hoped for promotion, but they *passed* him *by* in favour of a younger man.
I cannot *pass* this insult *by* without a protest.

pass down
  vt sep

= hand down

pass for
  vt insep

be accepted as; be taken for
。。。とみなされる，。。。で通る

In his day he *passed for* a great pianist.
With an accent like that he could quite easily *pass for* a German.

107

pass off
1 *vi*

disappear; end gradually
消える，なくなる

I am glad your headache *has passed off*.
The pain *will pass off* quickly when you have taken this medicine.

pass off
2 *vi*

take place; be completed
(うまく) 行く，行われる

We had expected a lot of trouble at that meeting, but fortunately it *passed off* very quietly.
The concert *passed off* quite smoothly.

pass off
3 *vt sep**

represent falsely as.
(人が) にせ者で通す

..He tried *to pass* himself *off* as a university lecturer.
He *passed* his companion *off* as a retired army officer.

pass on
1 *vi*

= pass away (1)

pass on
2 *vi*

move on; proceed
先へ進む，進む

We've discussed this subject long enough; I think we should *pass on* to a different one.
Let us *pass on* to the next item on the agenda, shall we?

pass on
3 *vt sep*

communicate; convey
伝える

Please *pass* this message *on* to the rest of your friends.
The news of the king's arrival *was passed on* by word of mouth.

pass out
vi

faint; lose consciousness
気絶する，意識を失う

People often *pass out* in crowded places.
She nearly *passed out* when she heard the news.

pass over
1 *vi*

= pass away (1)

pass over 2 *vt sep*	= pass by (2)
pass up *vt sep*	let slip; miss のがす，取り逃がす

You should never have *passed up* such a good deal.
She *passed up* a marvellous opportunity to become an actress.

EXERCISE 30

Use synonyms in place of the underlined phrasal verbs:

1 The demonstration passed off without incident.
2 He read the note and passed it on to his neighbour.
3 We waited for the funeral procession to pass by.
4 He speaks English well enough to pass for a native (*use the passive*).
5 She passed up a good chance to study abroad.
6 The legend has been passed down from father to son.
7 He passed away yesterday at dawn.
8 The intense heat of the sun made her pass out.
9 He tried to pass his secretary off as his wife.
10 We cannot pass over this incident without a formal protest.

PAY

pay back 1 *vt sep*	repay; pay in return 返す，払い戻す

She *paid back* the money she had borrowed from me.
I must *pay* Mr Jones *back* the £200 he lent me.
The loan will have *to be paid back* to the bank with 12% interest.

pay back 2 *vt sep*	retaliate; revenge oneself 仕返しをする，しっぺい返しをする

He *paid* her *back* for her infidelity* by going out with another woman.
I'll *pay* him *back* for this insult, you can be sure of that.

pay for
vt insep

be punished for
罰をうける，痛い目にあう，苦しむ

He *paid for* his rashness* with his life.
They made him *pay* dearly *for* it.

pay in(to)
vt sep

deposit in an account
(金を銀行口座などに) 払い込む

The young couple *paid in* all their savings *to* a building* society.
Please *pay* this sum *into* my partner's account.

pay off
1 *vi*

prove profitable
引き合う，利益をもたらす，成果をあげる

Buying second-hand machinery never *pays off* in the long run.
The scheme *has paid off* rather handsomely.

pay off
2 *vt sep*

recompense and dismiss from service
給料を払って解雇する

They *have paid off* fifty of their employees during this month alone.
The crew of the ship *were paid off* at the end of the voyage.

pay off
3 *vt sep*

settle (a debt etc.)
完済する

Have we *paid off* all our outstanding* debts yet?
It took him two full years *to pay* that loan *off*.

pay out
1 *vt sep*

disburse; hand out (money)
支払う

We've had *to pay out* an awful lot of money this year on repairs to that house.
The cashier *pays* the salaries *out* at the end of each month.

pay out
2 *vt sep*

= pay back (2)

pay up *vi*	pay money owed in full 皆済する、全額払い込む

Unless you *pay up* we shall have to take you to court.
Since we have no other choice, we might as well *pay up*.

EXERCISE 31

Fill in the blank spaces with the correct prepositions or particles. In some examples more than one answer is possible:

1 Don't you think it's time you paid him ... the money you owe him?
2 He'll have to pay ... this stupid mistake.
3 He received a cheque for £100 and paid it ... to the bank.
4 She paid him ... for the wrong he had done her.
5 It was a risky thing to do, but it paid ... in the end.
6 He paid his servants ... because they were not needed any longer.
7 I think you ought to pay ... and be grateful to him for lending you the money in the first place.
8 The government pays ... millions of pounds each year in unemployment* benefits.

PULL

pull about *vt sep**	maltreat; handle roughly 引っ張り回す、乱暴に扱う

I wish you would stop *pulling* your children *about* like that.

pull back *vi, vt sep*	(cause to) withdraw or retreat 撤退する、退去させる

It's doubtful whether they will ever *pull back* from the land captured in the last war.
The commander *pulled* his men *back* under cover of darkness.

pull down 1 *vt sep*	draw downwards 引き下ろす、下に引く

She *pulled down* the blinds to keep the sun out.

pull down 2 *vt sep*	demolish 取り壊す
	They *pulled down* the derelict* house and built a garage in its place. Many old buildings *are being pulled down* these days.
pull down 3 *vt sep**	weaken; debilitate 弱らせる
	A bad attack of flu *has pulled* him *down* a lot. She looks a bit *pulled down* by her recent illness.
pull in(to) 1 *vi, vt insep*	(of a train) enter a station (列車が駅に) 入る
	The Orient Express *pulled in* dead on time. It was close upon midnight when we *pulled into* Paddington.
pull in(to) 2 *vi, vt insep*	(of a vehicle) draw to a halt at the roadside (車が) 道路わきに寄る，止まる
	Suddenly the car *pulled in* to the side of the road. On our way to Cambridge we *pulled into* a lay-by* for some coffee.
pull off 1 *vt sep*	remove with force (衣服などを) 急いで脱ぐ，取りはずす
	He *pulled off* his jumper and started digging the garden. She *pulled* her gloves *off* and placed them on the table.
pull off 2 *vt sep*	succeed in achieving sth. difficult うまくやってのける
	You can rely on him to *pull off* the deal. We *have pulled* it *off*; we have won the championship.
pull on *vt sep*	don; put on (服を) 着る，(くつ下を) 履く
	She *pulled on* a jumper over her shirt. He *pulled* his boots *on* and hurried off to school.

pull out
1 *vi*

(of a train) leave a station
(列車などが) 出て行く

The train *pulled out* half an hour late.
Our connection to Istanbul *was pulling out* of platform six as we ran into the station.

pull out
2 *vi*

withdraw (from)
手を引く，やめる

If you don't *pull out* now you'll regret it later.
They decided *to pull out* of the bargain at the very last minute.

pull out
3 *vt sep*

extract
抜く

Take the pincers* and *pull* those nails *out*.
He has gone to the dentist to have a bad tooth *pulled out*.

pull over
vi

move to the side of the road
(車を) 道路の片側に寄せる

The lorry driver *pulled over* to let us pass.
The car ahead of us suddenly *pulled over* and stopped.

pull through
*vi, vt sep**

recover; help recover
全快する，切り抜けさせる

He was seriously injured, but managed *to pull through*.
She was critically ill in hospital, but good doctors and careful nursing *pulled* her *through*.

pull together
1 *vi*

co-operate; work in harmony
協力して働く，力を合わせる

After this crushing defeat, the Party needs *to pull together* more than ever before.
We can come through this crisis if we all *pull together*.

pull together
2 *vt sep**

(with reflexive pronoun) compose oneself
気を落ちつける，元気を取り戻す

The girl had been crying, but *pulled* herself *together* when she saw me coming.
Please, George, *pull* yourself *together*.

pull up
1 *vi, vt sep*

(cause to) stop
止まる，止める

The car suddenly *pulled up* and two men with pistols leapt out.
He *pulled up* his car opposite the building and waited.

pull up
2 *vt sep*

uproot; pluck
引き抜く

The gardener *pulled up* the weeds from the flower-beds.
He *pulled* the tree *up* by the roots.

pull up
3 *vt sep**

rebuke; reprimand
しかる，懲戒する

She *pulled* her son *up* for answering her back.
Those children ought *to be pulled up* about their bad manners.

EXERCISE 32

Fill in the blank spaces with the correct prepositions or particles:

1 It was getting on for one o'clock when we pulled ... Euston.
2 A lot of old houses are being pulled ... and replaced by modern blocks of flats.
3 The troops pulled ... to prepared lines of defence.
4 I should like to know who pulled ... those plants.
5 Will you help me pull ... these tight boots, please?
6 He was sharply pulled ... for his rude remarks.
7 The doctor assured me that she would pull ... all right.
8 You know I hate being pulled ... like that, so stop it.
9 Pull yourself ..., man!
10 The driver pulled ... at the traffic lights and waited.
11 He has managed to pull ... yet another important business deal.
12 You'd better pull ... before it's too late.

13 The family has always pulled ... in difficult times like these.
14 The policeman signalled to the driver to pull ... to the side of the road.
15 It was so cold outside he hurried to pull ... a warm sweater.

PUT

put about
  vt sep

spread; circulate
広める

Somebody has been *putting* rumours *about* that we are getting engaged.
It was *put about* that she was having an affair with her driving instructor.

put across
  *vt sep**

communicate; explain
(考えなどを) 理解させる，わからせる

The teacher knows his stuff well, but he can't *put* it *across* (to the class).
How can we best *put* our manifesto *across* to the electorate*?

put aside
1 *vt sep*

place to one side
(一時) わきへやる

She *put aside* her sewing to rest her eyes for a few minutes.
Put your book *aside* and listen to me carefully.

put aside
2 *vt sep*

ignore; disregard
無視する，忘れる

I can't *put aside* the fact that the man once committed a murder.
In times of national crisis, party differences *should be put aside*.

put aside
3 *vt sep*

save
取っておく

We've managed *to put aside* enough money for a holiday this summer.
I have a few hundred pounds *put aside* for emergencies.

put away　　　　put in the proper place
1 *vt sep*　　　　（いつもの所へ）しまう，片付ける

　　　　　　　　Don't leave your things about; *put* them *away*.
　　　　　　　　Put those papers *away* in your drawers.

put away　　　　confine (esp. in a mental home)
2 *vt sep*　　　　（精神病院などに）入れる

　　　　　　　　The authorities *put* him *away* for assaulting* harmless old ladies.
　　　　　　　　A man like that deserves *to be put away* for life.

put away　　　　devour; eat copiously
3 *vt sep*　　　　（飲食物を）平らげる

　　　　　　　　You would be surprised at the amount of food this child can *put away*.
　　　　　　　　She *put away* a huge breakfast before she left.

put away　　　　(of animals) put to death
4 *vt sep*　　　　（老犬，病気の動物などを）殺す，安楽死させる

　　　　　　　　We decided *to put away* that dog because it was suffering too much.
　　　　　　　　The horse broke a leg and had *to be put away*.

put away　　　　= put aside (3)
5 *vt sep*

put back　　　　replace; return
1 *vt sep*　　　　返す，（もとの所へ）戻す

　　　　　　　　Please *put* that dress *back* in the wardrobe.
　　　　　　　　Put that thing *back* where you found it.

put back　　　　move backwards
2 *vt sep*　　　　（時計の針を）戻す，遅らせる

　　　　　　　　The clock was ten minutes fast, so I *put* it *back*.
　　　　　　　　We *put* our watches *back* by an hour.

put back 3 *vt sep*	delay; hinder 遅らせる，。。。の進行を妨げる，（生産が）落ちる The miners' ban* on overtime *put back* production by 15%. This *will put* us *back* five years at least.
put by *vt sep*	= put aside (3)
put down 1 *vt sep*	place down 下に置く They *put down* the heavy box gently. *Put* that gun *down*, you idiot!
put down 2 *vt sep*	allow to alight; drop 降ろす Please *put* me *down* at the next junction. Ask the conductor *to put* you *down* at the Albert Hall.
put down 3 *vt sep*	suppress; crush; quell 押えつける，鎮圧する，鎮める The army *put down* the rebellion with ferocity*. The revolt* *was* savagely *put down*.
put down 4 *vt sep*	record; write down 記入する，書く If I don't *put down* his address in my diary, I'm certain to forget it. He wants everything *put down* on paper. The instructions *were put down* in black and white. Please *put* the drinks *down* to me/to my account.
put down 5 *vt sep*	= put away (4)
put down to *vt sep**	attribute to; ascribe to 。。。のせいにする，。。。が原因である I *put* his bad performance *down to* nerves. His poor health can be *put down to* malnutrition.

put forward
1 *vt sep*

move forward
(時計の針を) 進ませる

Your watch is a bit slow; *put* it *forward* to the correct time.
At the beginning of British summer time, clocks are *put forward* one hour.

put forward
2 *vt sep*

advance; offer for consideration
提言する，提案する

He *had put forward* lots of good suggestions.
The committee *has put forward* a series of proposals for settling the dispute.

put forward
3 *vt sep*

nominate; recommend
推薦する

He will *put* himself *forward* as a candidate at the next election.
His was one of the names *put forward* for promotion.

put in
1 *vt sep*

insert; add
入れる，付け加える

You'll have *to put in* four 10p pieces before you can start the machine.
This article is a bit too short. Why not *put in* a few more paragraphs?

put in
2 *vt sep*

devote; spend
(金，時を) 費やす，使う

He *has put in* a lot of work on that project.
How many hours do you have *to put in* on your French each day?

put in
3 *vi, vt insep*

apply; submit
申し込む，(書類などを) 提出する

He *put in* for that job, but they turned him down.
The manager *put in* an application for extra staff in his department.

put off 1 *vt sep*	postpone; defer 延期する，遅らせる	

Never *put off* till tomorrow what you can do today. (proverb)
We shall have *to put* the meeting *off* until after Easter.

put off 2 *vt sep*	discourage; deter 。。。の意欲（気力）をなくさせる	

She wanted to do that course, but the teacher *put* her *off* by saying how difficult it was.
Don't listen to any of that nonsense; he is only trying to *put* you *off*.

put off 3 *vt sep*	repel; cause to dislike 食欲を失わせる，うんざりさせる	

I don't like curry; the smell *puts* me *off*.
His bad breath *put* me *off* my meal.

put off 4 *vt sep*	extinguish; switch off 消す	

Don't forget *to put off* the lights before you go to bed.
Put that wireless *off*; I can't concentrate at all.

put off 5 *vt sep*	get rid of by delay or evasive shifts （口実などで）。。。から言い逃れをする	

He keeps *putting off* his creditors with promises.
I'm not going *to be put off* with excuses any longer.

put off 6 *vt sep*	disturb; distract 邪魔する，気を散らす	

Will you two keep quiet! You *are putting* me *off*.
The slightest thing can *put* him *off* when he is working.

put off 7 *vt sep*	= put down (2)	

put on 1 *vt sep*	don; dress in 着る，かぶる	

Take off that dirty shirt and *put on* a clean one.
The gentleman *put* his hat *on* when he left the house.

119

put on 2 *vt sep*	light; switch on (電気，ガス，テレビなどを) つける	

Put the electric fire *on*, please; I'm feeling a bit cold.
She *put on* the radio to listen to the news.

put on 3 *vt sep*	gain (weight) (体重を) 増す，太る	

She *put on* a lot of weight over the Christmas period.
He *put on* five kilos living in the country.

put on 4 *vt insep*	assume; affect (態度，外観を) 身につける，．．． の振りをする	

He *put on* a posh accent to impress his visitors.
It was obvious to everybody that her grief was only *put on*.

put on 5 *vt sep*	produce; stage 催す	

The schoolchildren *put on* a show for the Queen's visit.
We usually *put* a party *on* at the end of each term.

put out 1 *vt sep**	expel; throw out 外へ出す，追い出す	

If you don't keep quiet you'*ll be put out* at once.

put out 2 *vt sep*	extinguish 消す	

Remember *to put out* all the lights before you go out.
The child *put* the candle *out* by blowing at it.

put out 3 *vt sep**	(*usu. pass.*) upset; annoy 困らせる，いら立たせる	

He was very much *put out* by her rude remarks.
Your mother feels rather *put out* about this incident.

put out 4 *vt sep**	inconvenience or trouble (oneself) 。。。のために骨を折る，わざわざする
	Please don't *put* yourself *out* for me. He would never *put* himself *out* for anyone, not even for you.
put out 5 *vt sep*	dislocate （。。。の関節を）脱きゅうする
	She fell down the ladder and *put* her shoulder *out* badly.
put over *vt sep*	= put across
put through 1 *vt sep*	connect (by telephone) 電話をつなぐ
	If you will hold on, sir, I'll *put* you *through* to the manager. *Put* me *through* to the president. It's urgent.
put through 2 *vt sep*	conclude; complete やり遂げる，完了する
	I'm quite confident that he'*ll put* the deal *through* without any difficulty. We are hoping *to put* this scheme *through* by next March.
put together *vt sep*	assemble 組み立てる
	It's easier to take a clock apart than *to put* it *together* again.
put up 1 *vt sep*	raise （はしごを）掛ける，（手を）挙げる
	He *put up* the ladder and then took it down again. The pupil *put* his hand *up* to ask a question.

put up
2 *vt sep*

build; erect
建てる，（テントを）張る

They *have put up* tower-blocks all over the town.
He is going *to put* a tent *up* in his garden.

put up
3 *vi, vt sep*

lodge; give lodging to
宿泊させる，泊める

We *put up* at a guest-house for three nights.
Can you *put* me *up* for the night?
I shall be very glad *to put* you *up* when you come to London.

put up
4 *vt sep*

increase; raise
（値を）上げる

The banks *have put up* their interest rates by one per cent.
The landlady has twice *put* the rent *up* in the past twelve months.

put up
5 *vt insep*

provide; raise (money)
提供する，調達する

A generous benefactor* *put up* the money for the scheme.
You have only two days *to put up* the cash.

put up with
vt insep

tolerate; bear; endure
我慢する，耐える

I refuse *to put up with* his impertinence* any longer.
We have *to put up with* a lot of noise from the neighbours.

EXERCISE 33

A Replace the underlined words with phrasal verbs containing *put*. In some examples more than one answer is possible:

1 It took the firemen several hours to extinguish the blaze.
2 He has gained weight since he stopped smoking.
3 A statue of Admiral Nelson was erected after his death.
4 Let's postpone our visit to the museum till next week.
5 I won't tolerate any bad behaviour in this house.

6 The government intends to <u>increase</u> the price of petrol by 2p a gallon.
7 She <u>donned</u> her best dress for the occasion.
8 He has <u>advanced</u> some very convincing arguments in support of the idea.
9 The speaker didn't seem to be able to <u>explain</u> his views effectively.
10 He has <u>submitted</u> a claim for travel expenses.
11 You should look ahead and try to <u>save</u> something for your retirement.
12 The boy <u>assumed</u> an air of innocence when he was accused of breaking the window.
13 Troops were called out to <u>suppress</u> the rebellion.
14 Her face is enough to <u>repel</u>* anyone.
15 The accident was <u>attributed</u>* to careless driving.

B Fill in the blank spaces with the correct prepositions or particles:

1 Put your toys . . . , darling! It's time to go to bed.
2 Your watch is ten minutes fast; you'd better put it . . . .
3 We'll have to put him . . . until he finds somewhere to live.
4 I'll put you . . . to that extension if you will hold the line.
5 Put . . . the light, please; it's getting dark in here.
6 When you've finished with these books, remember to put them . . . on the shelf.
7 Someone has put the story . . . that the chairman is resigning.
8 I took the liberty of putting your name . . . on the list.
9 Don't put . . . your cigarette in the saucer; use the ash-tray.
10 Her husband knocks her about a lot. I'm surprised she puts . . . . . . it.

RUN

run across
vt insep

meet or find by chance
(人に) 偶然出会う, (物を) 偶然見つける

I *ran across* an old friend of mine in London yesterday.
Where did you *run across* these old coins?

run after
vt insep

chase; pursue
。。。のあとを追う, 追いまわす

The shopkeeper *ran after* the thief who had stolen some goods.
She has been *running after* him for years, but he isn't interested in her.

run along
vi

see *get along*, *run away* (2) example 2

run away
1 *vi*

escape; flee
逃げ出す，家出をする

The boys *ran away* when I shouted at them.
This is the third time he *has run away* from school.
At the age of fifteen he ran away from home and went to sea.

run away
2 *vi*

leave; go away
立ち去る，出て行く

Don't *run away*; I have something to show you.
Your daddy is busy, darling; *run away* and play in the garden.

run away with
1 *vt insep*

elope with
駆け落ちする

Their son *has run away with* the neighbour's daughter.
She *ran away with* her music teacher.

run away with
2 *vt insep*

steal and run away
持ち逃げする

While I was having coffee in the cafeteria, someone *ran away with* my luggage.
The cashier *has run away with* the company's money.

run away with
3 *vt insep*

consume; use up
使い尽くす

These big cars *run away with* a lot of petrol.
A project of this magnitude will *run away with* our funds.

run away with
4 *vt insep*

accept (an idea) too hastily
早合点して（ある考えを）いだく

Don't *run away with* the idea that you are indispensable*.

run away with 5 *vt insep*	gain complete control of （感情などが人を）駆りたてる	

He tends to let his temper *run away with* him.
Don't let your enthusiasm *run away with* you.

run away with 6 *vt insep*	win easily 圧倒的にまさって...を得る	

Their candidate *ran away with* the election.
The Chinese players *ran away with* the table-tennis tournament.

run back *vt sep*	re-wind (film, tape, etc.) （フイルム，テープを）巻き戻す	

I'll *run* the tape *back* when I've finished listening to it.
Can we have that bit of the film *run back*, please?

run down 1 *vi*	become unwound or discharged （ぜんまいが解けて時計などが）止まる （電池などが）切れる	

The clock *ran down* because I forgot to wind it.
The batteries seem to *have run down*.

run down 2 *vt sep*	knock down with a vehicle （自動車が人などを）ひく	

A careless driver *ran* her *down* as she was crossing the street.
He was *run down* by a taxi and was rushed to hospital.

run down 3 *vt sep*	disparage; speak ill of けなす，くさす	

He is always *running down* his colleagues behind their backs.

run down 4 *vt sep*	find; locate 追い詰める，捜し出す	

The police finally *ran* him *down* at a small hotel in Paris.
We've had an awful lot of trouble *running* her *down*.

run down
5 vt sep

(*pass.*) exhausted; debilitated
ひどく疲れる，衰弱する

You look terribly *run down*, George. I think you ought to take a long holiday.
I don't know what's the matter with me, but I feel completely *run down*.

run for
vt insep

be a candidate for
立侯補する

He *ran for* Mayor twice, but was unsuccessful on both occasions.
He has finally made up his mind *to run for* President.

run in
1 vt sep

drive (a new car) slowly and carefully to avoid straining the engine
(新車を) ならし運転する

If you want *to run in* your car properly you shouldn't exceed 35 miles an hour.
'*Running in*. Please pass.' (notice on the back window of a new car)

run in
2 vt sep

arrest; apprehend
(軽罪などで) 逮捕する

The police *ran* him *in* for indecent* exposure.
Brian *was run in* for speeding last night.

run into
1 vt insep

collide with
。。。と衝突する

She lost control of her car and *ran into* a stationary* van.
The two planes *ran into* each other on the runway.

run into
2 vt insep

meet by chance
。。。に偶然に会う

I *ran into* an old school friend on a visit to Edinburgh.

run into
3 vt insep

amount to; reach
。。。に達する

His annual income *runs into* five figures.
Her new book *has run into* three impressions* already.

run into 4 *vt insep*	be involved in 。。。に陥る
	You'll soon *run into* debt if you are not careful with your spending. I'm afraid your son *has run into* trouble with the headmaster.
run off with *vt insep*	= run away with (1), (2)
run out 1 *vi*	come to an end 使い尽くす，尽きる，終わる
	What are we going to do when our supply of food *runs out*? My patience is beginning *to run out*.
run out 2 *vi*	expire; terminate 満期になる，失効する
	My driving-licence *runs out* on November 18th. When does your contract *run out*?
run out of *vt insep*	exhaust; finish completely 使い果たす，切らす，なくなる
	We *ran out of* petrol in the middle of nowhere. We *are running out of* time, gentlemen! I *have run out of* ideas; I can't think of anything.
run over 1 *vi, vt insep*	overflow （液体，容器が）あふれる，こぼれる
	I forgot to turn off the taps in the bath, and the water *ran over*. The milk *has run* all *over* the floor.
run over 2 *vt insep*	recapitulate; rehearse 繰り返す，。。。にざっと目を通す
	I'll just *run over* the main points of the lesson again. Let us *run over* that bit once more, shall we?

run over 3 *vt sep*	go over while driving (車が人などを）ひく

Look out! You nearly *ran over* that woman.
He *was run over* by a car and killed instantly.

run through 1 *vt insep*	read or examine quickly 通読する，．．．にざっと目を通す

Just *run through* this essay and tell me what you think of it.
The teacher *ran through* his notes before starting the lesson.

run through 2 *vt insep*	spend completely; squander (財産などを）使い尽くす，浪費する

He has already *run through* the money he inherited from his uncle.
She *ran through* the fortune in less than a year.

run through 3 *vt sep**	impale; pierce (剣などで相手を）刺す

He *ran* his enemy *through* with a sword.
The sentries* *were run through* with spears.

run to 1 *vt insep*	amount to; reach ．．．に達する，及ぶ

The repair bill *will run to* several thousand pounds.
His dissertation* *runs to* approximately four hundred pages.

run to 2 *vt insep*	be sufficient for; afford ．．．の能力（財力）をもっている，十分足りる

My salary won't *run to* eating in expensive restaurants.
I can't possibly *run to* a new colour TV.

run up 1 *vt sep*	raise; hoist (旗などを）揚げる

The besieged garrison *ran up* a white flag as a sign of surrender.

run up
2 *vt sep*

accumulate
(出費，借金などを) 急にためる

She *ran up* a large bill at the butcher's.
You *have run up* an awful lot of debts already.

run up
3 *vt sep*

sew quickly
大急ぎで縫う

My sister *ran up* that blouse for me this morning.
It shouldn't take long *to run up* this dress.

run up against
vt insep

encounter; meet with
。。。に衝突する，。。。に出くわす

We did not expect *to run up against* that kind of opposition.
He *has run up against* all sorts of problems.

EXERCISE 34

A Fill in the blank spaces with the correct prepositions or particles. In some examples more than one answer is possible.

1 We have run ...... sugar. Will you go and buy some?
2 Don't run ...... the idea that you can go on breaking the rules.
3 She was run ... by a cyclist and broke her arm.
4 He is looking a bit run ... after his illness.
5 Two small boys ran ...... my handbag and disappeared in the crowd.
6 I ran ... Hilda at a fun-fair the other day.
7 She is inclined to let her imagination run ...... her.
8 The car skidded* and ran ... the back of a lorry.
9 It's almost impossible to run ... from this prison.
10 The budget* just won't run ... caviare every day.
11 My wife is running ... accounts at five different shops.
12 You will ruin your car if you do not run it ... properly.

B Use synonyms in place of the underlined phrasal verbs:

1 She is always <u>running</u> her neighbours <u>down</u>.
2 The police <u>ran him in</u> for dangerous driving.
3 Let us just <u>run through</u> this part one more time.
4 This is just one of the obstacles* we expect to <u>run up against</u>.
5 She <u>ran off with</u> a man old enough to be her father.

6 The policeman <u>ran after</u> the thief, but could not catch him.
7 The present agreement <u>runs out</u> in June.
8 This scheme will simply <u>run away with</u> our money.
9 It took me the whole afternoon to <u>run down</u> the reference.
10 Time is <u>running out</u>, and so we must hurry.
11 Don't put too much water in the tank, or it'll <u>run over</u>.
12 She has already <u>run through</u> the fortune she won on the pools.

SEE

see about
vt insep

attend to; deal with (see *see to*)
。。。のことを考える，手段を講じる

When are you going *to see about* those bills? They should have been paid a month ago, you know!
We must *see about* decorating the spare room for auntie's visit.

see into
vt insep

investigate; inquire into
調査する

He promised that he would *see into* the matter at once.
Perhaps you wouldn't mind *seeing into* it for me then?

see off
1 *vt sep**

accompany sb. to his point of departure
見送る

They have gone to the airport *to see* their daughter *off*.
He *was seen off* by some of his relatives and close friends.

see off
2 *vt sep**

cause to leave
追い払う

I don't like those men hanging about the place; please *see* them *off* (the premises*).

see out
1 *vt sep.**

conduct to the door
玄関まで見送る

Miss Brown, *will* you *see* this lady *out*, please?
Don't bother to get up; I can *see* myself *out*.

see out
2 vt sep*

live or last until a specified period has elapsed
(時が経過するまで) 生き抜く, 続く

It's doubtful whether he *will see* another week *out*.
Do we have enough coal *to see* the winter *out*?

see over
   vt insep

inspect
見回る, 検分する

They went *to see over* the house yesterday, but they didn't find it very attractive.

see through
1 vt insep

understand the true nature of sb. or his dubious intentions
。. 。の真相を見抜く

She thought she could fool me, but I *saw through* her game immediately.
I *saw through* him at once. I knew exactly what he was after.

see through
2 vt sep*

bring to a conclusion
うまくやってのける

We are still hoping that you will be able *to see* the work *through* by next spring.
You can rely on him *to see* this thing *through*.

see through
3 vt sep*

help sb. through a difficult time
(難局などを乗り切るまで人を) 助ける

He had always trusted that his friends *would see* him *through* when he was in trouble.
I hope this small cheque *will see* you *through*.

see to
   vt insep

attend to; take care of
気を付ける, (処置するように) 計らう, 直す

I'*ll see to* it you receive the cheque within the next few days.
See to it that Mr Freeman is not disturbed.
The lift has broken down again. Have it *seen to* at once.

131

EXERCISE 35

Fill in the blank spaces with the correct prepositions or particles. In some examples more than one answer is possible:

1. I'll do the washing-up if you'll see . . . the dinner.
2. A good host always sees his guests . . . when they leave.
3. You are leaving tomorrow, are you? I'll come and see you . . . at the station.
4. You must see . . . booking seats for the play before they are sold out.
5. Take the dog and see those trespassers . . . my land.
6. I'm not such a fool, you know! I can see . . . your clever plans.
7. A party of foreign visitors came to see . . . the factory this morning.
8. They are determined to see their struggle . . . right to the end.
9. I wonder whether granny will see the month . . . . She looks very ill.
10. We are seeing . . . the question of extending his contract for a further six months.

SET

set about 1 *vt insep*	begin; tackle 始める，．．．に取り掛かる	

They *set about* their work eagerly.
He doesn't have the slightest idea of how *to set about* the job.
As soon as the ship entered dock they *set about* unloading the cargo.

set about 2 *vt insep*	attack 攻撃する，なぐりつける	

The two boys *set about* each other fiercely.
The policemen *set about* some demonstrators with their clubs.

set apart *vt sep**	cause to stand out 目立たせる	

His intelligence *sets* him *apart* from the rest of the class.

set aside 1 *vt sep*	place to one side 片側に置く She *set aside* her knitting when I came into the room. He *set* his paper *aside* and listened to what she had to say.
set aside 2 *vt sep*	disregard; dismiss 取り除く，無視する You must look at this objectively and *set aside* your personal feelings. The speaker *set aside* all objections made by some people in the audience.
set aside 3 *vt sep*	annul; quash 無効にする，破棄する The appeal court *set aside* the judgement of the lower court. The verdict of the jury *was set aside* and the death sentence commuted*.
set aside 4 *vt sep*	see *put aside/by*
set back 1 *vt sep*	move backwards 遅らせる，（時計の針を）戻す He *set back* the hands of the clock one hour.
set back 2 *vt sep*	hinder; delay (進歩などを) 妨げる，遅らせる The continuing industrial disputes could *set back* our economic recovery considerably. This *will set* us *back* some years.
set back 3 *vt sep**	cost ．．．のため．．．の費用がかかる His birthday party *set* him *back* hundreds of pounds. That new car must *have set* him *back* quite a bit.
set down 1 *vt sep*	allow to alight; drop 降ろす The taxi *set* us *down* just opposite the museum. Could you please *set* me *down* at the next set of lights?

set down
2 *vt sep*

record; write down
書き留める

He asked me *to set* everything *down* on paper.
The instructions *were set down* in black and white.

set forth
vt sep

expound; give an account of
述べる，説明する

The minister *set forth* his views with clarity and force.
The Liberal leader *set forth* the policies of his party in an interview with newspaper reporters.

set in
vi

begin; start
始まる

Winter *set in* rather early this year.
The rain seems *to have set in* for the night.

set off
1 *vi*

depart; begin a journey
出発する

We intend *to set off* tomorrow at dawn.
They *have set off* on an expedition to the Antarctic.
They *set off* for Australia in great haste.

set off
2 *vt sep*

cause to explode
（花火を）打ち上げる，（火薬などを）爆発させ・

Some boys *were setting off* fireworks in the street.
The terrorists *set* a bomb *off* outside the shopping precinct.

set off
3 *vt sep*

cause to start
（事を）ひき起こす，（人に..)させる

His latest book *has set off* a fierce controversy.*
That remark *set* everybody *off* laughing.

set off
4 *vt sep*

intensify or improve by contrast
引き立たせる，美しくする

This ring, madam, *will set off* your hand beautifully.
Her black hair *was set off* by the red dress she was wearing.

set on *vt insep*		attack 襲う

As he was walking down the street one night, two men suddenly *set on* him and knocked him senseless.
He *was set on* and beaten up by a gang of boys.

set out
1 *vi*

= set off (1)

set out
2 *vi*

have as an intention or goal
(。。。することを）企てる，。。。しようとする

She *set out* to become the first woman prime minister.
This article *sets out* to prove that smoking is the main cause of lung cancer.

set out
3 *vt sep*

state; explain
述べる，説明する

He *set out* his arguments in a remarkably convincing way.
The Liberals *have set out* their conditions for supporting the government in tomorrow's no-confidence vote.

set out
4 *vt sep*

organize; display
まとめ上げる，並べる

You haven't *set out* your essay very well, I'm afraid.
The goods *were* neatly *set out* on the stalls.

set to
1 *vi*

begin to work vigorously
(仕事に懸命に）取り掛かる

They *set to* and finished the job in no time at all.

set to
2 *vi*

begin to fight or argue
けんかを始める

The two men *set to* with their fists.

set up 1 *vi*		start a business （事業，商売を）始める
		At the end of the war, his father moved to Bournemouth where he *set up* as an inn-keeper.

set up 2 *vt sep*		erect; place in position （まっすぐに）据える，建てる
		He *set up* a hot-dog stall outside the football stadium. The army *set up* an observation post at the top of the hill.

set up 3 *vt sep*		establish; institute 設立する，設ける，（調査を）始める
		The government *has set up* a commission* to examine the country's educational system. An inquiry into the causes of the air crash *was set up* by the airline officials.

set up 4 *vi, vt sep**		claim to be 。。。だと主張する
		I do not *set up* to be an expert in this field. He *sets* himself *up* as an authority on fossils.*

set up 5 *vt sep*		achieve (a record) （記録などを）打ち立てる
		The Russian athletes *set up* several new records at the last Olympic Games.

set up 6 *vt sep*		provide; equip 供給する，用意する，支度してやる
		His parents *set* him *up* with the necessary books for college. The children *have been set up* with all the clothes they need.

EXERCISE 36

Fill in the blank spaces with the correct prepositions or particles. In some examples more than one answer is possible:

1. Ask the driver to set you ... at the Odeon.
2. They set ... their reasons for refusing to support the motion.
3. The League* of Nations was set ... in 1919.
4. This frame will set ... your painting very nicely.
5. A rare talent set Shakespeare ... from other Elizabethan poets.
6. We must get the shed fixed before the bad weather sets ....
7. They have been set ... with all the provisions they need for the voyage.
8. I don't know how to set ... a job like this.
9. He set ... to break the world record for the high jump.
10. We set ... at five and reached our destination before sunset.
11. The dinner set me ... eight quid*.
12. The policeman set ... in writing all the statements we made.
13. A gang of hooligans* set ... him and injured him very badly.
14. The recent outbreaks of violence could set ... the peace efforts considerably.
15. He gave up his job at the factory and set ... as a greengrocer.

SHOW

show (a)round
vt sep

take sb. round a place
人に場所を案内して回る

I'd love *to show* you *around* the city.
We *were shown round* the factory by the director himself.

show in(to)
vt sep

usher into a place
案内する，(客などを) 通す

When Mr Francis arrives *show* him *in* at once.
The secretary *showed* me *into* the manager's office.
We *were shown into* a large drawing-room by the butler*.

show off
1 *vi*

boast; behave ostentatiously
(力量，学問などを) 見せびらかす，
仰仰しく振り舞う

He just can't help *showing off* in public.
I wish you would stop *showing off*, William!

137

show off 2 *vt sep*	exhibit; display 引き立たせる，よく見せる

This dress *shows off* your figure very nicely.
The gold frame *shows* the painting *off* well.

show off 3 *vt sep*	display ostentatiously 見せびらかす

She went to the dance just *to show off* her new clothes.
She likes *to show* her daughter *off*, doesn't she?

show out *vt sep*	conduct to the door （人を）外に送り出す

Miss Perkins, will you *show* this gentleman *out*, please?
The guests *were shown out* by the maid.

show up 1 *vi*	arrive; appear （会合などに）顔を見せる，来る

I can't understand why she hasn't *shown up* yet.
He never *shows up* on time for these meetings.
Only twenty people *showed up* at the party.

show up 2 *vt sep*	expose; unmask （欠点などを）暴露する，ばらす

He obviously enjoys *showing up* other people's mistakes.
They *showed* him *up* to be an impostor*.

show up 3 *vt sep*	embarrass; shame 恥ずかしい思いをさせる

If you don't stop *showing* me *up* in public I'll never go with you anywhere.

EXERCISE 37

Fill in the blank spaces with the correct prepositions or particles:

1 I waited for her for nearly one hour, but she didn't show ....
2 Don't keep the young lady waiting. Show her ....
3 The guide showed the tourists ... the ancient cathedral.
4 He'll probably stop showing ... if we don't take any notice of him.
5 My secretary will show you .... It's easy to get lost in this big building.

6 He keeps using French words just to show ... his knowledge of the language.
7 You shouldn't have shown your mother ... in front of all those people.

STAND

stand about
vi

stand idly in a certain place
(何もしないで）ぼんやり立っている

He kept us *standing about* for hours.
I wish you would stop *standing about* and do something useful instead.

stand around
vi

= stand about

stand aside
1 *vi*

get out of the way
わきえ寄る

Will you please *stand aside* and let me pass.

stand aside
2 *vi*

take no part; do nothing
傍観する，かまわない

We can't *stand aside* and let him do it all by himself.
Surely you don't expect me *to stand aside* and allow this thing to happen.

stand back
vi

stand clear
離れて立つ，後ろへ下がる

The firemen ordered the spectators *to stand back*.
Will everybody please *stand back*!

stand by
1 *vi*

be a mere bystander
そばにいて見物する

Several people *stood by* while the two men were fighting.
We cannot *stand* idly *by* and watch people die of starvation.

stand by 2 *vi*	be in a state of readiness 待ち構える，待機する Police were ordered *to stand by* for action. Other troops *are standing by* to help. *Stand by* for further instructions.
stand by 3 *vt insep*	support; remain loyal to 援助する，忠誠を尽くす，力になる He had always *stood by* his friends whenever they were in trouble. They *stood by* one another through* thick and thin.
stand by 4 *vt insep*	keep; adhere to; abide by 守る，固守する He is not the sort of man who *stands by* his promises. We've signed the agreement and we'*ll* just *have to stand by* it.
stand down 1 *vi*	leave the witness box 証人席から降りる The magistrate asked the witness *to stand down*. You may *stand down* now!
stand down 2 *vi*	withdraw (in favour of sb. else) (候補を譲って）身を引く，辞退する The candidate has offered *to stand down* in favour of a younger man. He is not going *to stand down* for anybody.
stand for 1 *vt insep*	represent; mean 。。。を表わす，。。。を意味する USSR *stands for* Union of Soviet Socialist Republics. The letters RAF *stand for* Royal Air Force.
stand for 2 *vt insep*	(*usu. neg.*) tolerate; permit 我慢する，黙認する Father wouldn't *stand for* any of that nonsense. I won't *stand for* his impudence any longer.

stand for 3 *vt insep*	advocate; contend for 唱導する，．．．のために戦う

Abraham Lincoln *stood for* the abolition of slavery in the United States.
He *has* always *stood for* racial equality.

stand for 4 *vt insep*	be a candidate for 立候補する

He *stood for* Parliament in 1970, but was not elected.
At the last election he *stood for* Bristol.

stand in for *vt insep*	take the place of 代役をする，．．．に代わる

He *had to stand in for* the actor who had been taken ill.
Will you *stand in for* me while I go out to the bank to cash a cheque?

stand off *vi*	keep at a distance 遠ざかっている

The two ships *were standing off* from each other.
The fleet *stood off* from the shore.

stand out *vi*	be conspicuous; be prominent 目立つ

The mosque *stood out* clearly against the sky.
He *stood out* from his contemporaries* by virtue* of his exceptional talents.

stand out against *vt insep*	persist in opposition or resistance あくまでも反抗（抵抗）する

The students *are standing out against* any further cuts in their grants*.
It takes courage *to stand out against* intimidation*.

stand over 1 *vi*	wait; be postponed 延期する

The last item on the agenda *will have to stand over* until our next meeting.

stand over
2 *vt insep*

watch closely
近くにいて見張る，監督する

I *have to stand over* him to make sure he studies.
Unless you *stand over* him he'll make a mess of the job.

stand up
vi

rise to the feet
起立する

The pupils *stood up* when the headmaster entered the classroom.
You can see better if you *stand up*.

stand up for
vt insep

defend; support
擁護する

Do you always *stand up for* your rights?
I hope you are not going *to stand up for* that rogue*.

stand up to
1 *vt insep*

withstand; resist
。。。に耐える

Steel *stands up to* heat better than other metals.
These shoes *will stand up to* a lot of wear and tear.

stand up to
2 *vt insep*

face boldly
勇敢に立ち向かう

Stop behaving like a coward and *stand up to* him.
She *would stand up to* the devil himself.

EXERCISE 38

A Replace the underlined words with phrasal verbs containing *stand*:

1 We dislike Nazism and all that it represents.
2 An honest man always keeps his word.
3 This matter will have to wait until later.
4 He says he is willing to withdraw if you want the job.
5 I won't tolerate this sort of behaviour.
6 Robin is taking the place of the player who has broken his leg.
7 He resisted all attempts to persuade him to change his mind.
8 What does the abbreviation *A.D.* mean?
9 These children need someone to watch them closely all the time; otherwise they never do any work.
10 This type of machine can withstand* even the roughest treatment.

B Fill in the blank spaces with the correct prepositions or particles:
1 Don't be afraid of standing . . . . . . that bully*.
2 Do you mean to say that you just stood . . . and watched the girl drown?
3 He is thinking of standing . . . mayor at the next municipal election.
4 The pilot was instructed to stand . . . and wait for final clearance before take-off.
5 She just stood . . . doing nothing while I did all the cleaning.
6 He stood . . . and let the others decide the question.
7 All our friends stood . . . us when we most needed them.
8 Mother would always stand . . . . . . Robert if any of us criticized him.
9 The judge asked the witness to stand . . . when he had finished giving evidence.
10 He stands . . . in a crowd because of his height and bald head.

TAKE

be taken aback
vt sep*
be startled; be surprised
びっくりする，驚く

When I saw him lying so still I *was* quite *taken aback*. I really thought he was dead.
We *were* all *taken aback* by the news of his resignation.

take after
vt insep
resemble; behave like
。。。に似る，。。。のように振る舞う

These children really *take after* their mother.
You certainly seem *to take after* your grandfather; he was very obstinate*, too.

take apart
vt sep*
dismantle; take to pieces
分解する，ばらばらにする

He *took* the radio *apart* and then put it together again.
The mechanic *took* the engine *apart* before repairing it.

take aside
vt sep*
take to one side
(人を) わきへ連れ出す

Take the girl *aside* and break the news gently.
He *took* me *aside* and whispered a few words in my ear about a proposed deal.

take away　　　remove
1 *vt sep*　　　　片付ける，取り去る，取り上げる

　　　　　　I won't need this ladder again; please *take* it *away*.
　　　　　　Take the knife *away* from that boy before he hurts himself.
　　　　　　In the reading rooms, books are not *to be taken away*.

take away　　　subtract
2 *vt sep*　　　　引く

　　　　　　Take away 4 from 9 and you get 5.
　　　　　　9 *take away* 4 is 5.

take back　　　return
1 *vt sep*　　　　返す

　　　　　　Will you do me a favour, Jim? *Take* these books *back* (to the library).

take back　　　agree to receive back
2 *vt sep*　　　　引き取る

　　　　　　The shirt which you sold me is too small. Will you *take* it *back*?
　　　　　　The shopkeeper refused *to take back* the rotten eggs.

take back　　　retract; withdraw
3 *vt sep*　　　　撤回する，取り消す

　　　　　　I *take back* what I said yesterday, and I hope you will accept my apology.
　　　　　　When she found out the truth, she came to me and *took* her remarks *back*.

take back　　　remind of earlier times
4 *vt sep**　　　昔を思い起こさせる

　　　　　　Those pictures *took* me *back* to the war.
　　　　　　This kind of music *does take* one *back*, doesn't it?

take down
1 *vt sep*

get or remove from a high level
降ろす

She reached up to the top shelf and *took down* an atlas.
He *took down* all the pictures from the walls when the room was being painted.

take down
2 *vt sep*

demolish; pull down
取り壊す

We are going *to take down* that partition and convert* the two small rooms into one big flat.

take down
3 *vt sep*

record; write down
記録する，書き取る

The policeman *took down* all the statements I made.
You are not supposed *to take down* every word I say.

take down
4 *vt sep*

dismantle
取り除く

The builders *took down* the scaffolding* round the building.

take down
5 *vt sep**

humble; humiliate
へこます，恥をかかせる

That young fellow is always bragging* about himself; he needs *to be taken down* a peg or two.

take for
*vt sep**

believe or assume to be
。。。だと思う

I *took* her *for* her sister; they are very much alike.
Who *do* you *take* me *for*?
Do you *take* me *for* a fool?

take from
vt insep

detract from
(名誉，評判などを) 落とす

He may have been a Nazi, but that doesn't *take from* his achievement as a physicist.

145

take in 1 *vt sep*	receive and accomodate; shelter 泊める，（下宿人を）置く，保護する The Joneses earn a bit of extra money by *taking in* lodgers. They *took* the stray* dog *in* and fed him.
take in 2 *vt sep*	make narrower (a garment) (衣服などの）丈を詰める，小さくする She has lost so much weight that she *had to take in* all her dresses. These trousers need *taking in* a little at the waist.
take in 3 *vt insep*	cover; comprise 含める，入れる This package tour *takes in* five Mediterranean countries. Greater London *takes in* parts of several counties.
take in 4 *vt sep*	understand; grasp 理解する，捕える He is so dull-witted* that he can't *take in* even the most straightforward speech. Did you *take in* what the man said? I didn't.
take in 5 *vt sep*	deceive; trick; cheat だます You really think you can *take* me *in* with your silly stories. The poor woman *was taken in* by the salesman and got nothing worth the money she had paid.
take off 1 *vi*	(of a plane) leave the ground 離陸する The aircraft crashed five minutes after it *had taken off*. We *took off* from Heathrow Airport at 9.30 p.m.

take off 2 *vt sep*	remove 脱ぐ

She hurriedly *took off* her coat and sank into an armchair.
Take that dirty jacket *off* and put on a clean one.
He *took off* his hat when he came into the house.

take off 3 *vt sep*	deduct (see *knock off*) （値段などを）引く

I'll stick my neck* out and *take off* five pounds just for you.
The shopkeeper *took* ten per cent *off* the bill, because I paid him in cash.

take off 4 *vt sep*	mimic; imitate （人の癖を）まねる

The comedian *took off* several well-known politicians during his act.
Alice *takes* the headmistress *off* to perfection.

take on 1 *vt sep*	employ; hire; engage 雇う

As they couldn't finish the work on time, they *had to take on* extra employees.
We can't *take on* any more staff, simply because we don't have the money for it.

take on 2 *vt sep*	accept; undertake 引き受ける

I'm sorry to have to disappoint you, but I can't *take on* any more work this week.
You should never *have taken* this job *on* in the first place.

take on 3 *vt sep*	accept as an opponent 。。。と対戦（対決）する

He is ready *to take on* anybody at chess.
I *took* Jim *on* at billiards and beat him.

take on acquire; assume
4 *vt insep* 取る，示す

This word is beginning *to take on* a new meaning.
Her face *took on* an angry look when I said that her hat did not suit her.

take out escort sb. somewhere for exercise or recreation
1 *vt sep** 連れ出す

The nurse *takes* the children *out* every day.
He *took* his girlfriend *out* to a discotheque.
I usually *take* the dog *out* for a walk after supper.

take out extract; pull out
2 *vt sep* 抜く

That tooth has given you so much pain. Why not see a dentist and *have* it *taken out*
She was admitted to hospital last Monday and had her appendix* *taken out*.

take out remove (stains, etc.)
3 *vt sep* （しみなどを）取る

This new washing-powder is very good for *taking out* all kinds of stains.

take out obtain; apply for and get
4 *vt sep* （免許などを）取る

You'll *have to take out* a driving-licence before you can drive the car.
You must *take out* an insurance policy, for the sake of your family.

take out vent; get rid of
5 *vt sep** 当たり散らす

I appreciate that you're having a difficult time, but please don't *take* your temper *out* on me.
She *took* her rage *out* on the poor dog.

take over
  vi, vt insep

assume control of
引き継ぐ

You've done your share of the work; now it's my turn *to take over* (from you).
When the father died, his eldest son *took over* the management of the property.
The army overthrew the old monarch and *took over* power.

take to
  1 *vt insep*

become fond of; like
好きになる

I *took to* that girl the moment I saw her.
I did watch bull-fighting on a couple of occasions, but I don't think I could ever *take to* it.

take to
  2 *vt insep*

seek refuge in
。。。に乗り移る，。。。に逃げ込む

Robin Hood *took to* the woods when he was made an outlaw*.
The crew could not keep the ship afloat and *took to* the life boats.

take to
  3 *vt insep*

get into the habit of
。。。するようになる，。。。する癖がつく

He *took to* gambling when he was young and never got out of it.
Our new teacher *has taken to* wearing jeans.

take up
  1 *vt sep*

shorten (a garment) (*cf. let down*)
（衣類を）縮める，詰める

These trousers are too long; get the tailor *to take* them *up*.
The dress does fit you nicely, but it needs *to be taken up* an inch or so.

take up
  2 *vt sep*

occupy; fill
（時間，場所などを）取る

Her charity work *takes up* most of her spare time.
I think we should sell that cupboard; it *takes up* too much room.

take up 3 *vt sep*	raise, discuss (問題点などを）持ち出す，相談する

I shall certainly *take* this matter *up* with the minister himself.

take up 4 *vt insep*	adopt the practice or study of (仕事，研究などを）始める

When my father retired, he *took up* gardening.
I'm thinking of *taking up* medicine when I finish secondary school.

take up 5 *vt insep*	resume; continue 再び始める，続ける

He *took up* the tale from where he had left off.

take up with *vt insep*	begin to associate with 。。。と交際する

I'm afraid your daughter *has taken up with* a bad lot*.
We don't want our son *to take up with* those boys because they are bad company.

EXERCISE 39

A Fill in the blank spaces with the correct prepositions or particles:

1 He did not recognize me in the dark and took me ... a thief.
2 She took ... her shoes before lying down on the bed.
3 The new director will take ... on January 12th.
4 He took his fiancée ... to dinner on her birthday.
5 The watchmaker took the clock ... before mending it.
6 His arrogant* behaviour had annoyed me for so long that I finally decided to take him ....
7 This new sweater of yours has a big hole in it. I'd take it ... to the shop if I were you.
8 He took ... life in the army like a duck to water.
9 Many old buildings are being taken ... and replaced by modern ones.
10 He took ... a patent in order to protect his invention.
11 The lecture was too difficult for me to take ....
12 I think you ought to take ... French; it'll help you a lot in your career.

B Replace the underlined words with phrasal verbs containing *take*:

1 He had a row* with his boss and <u>vented</u> his anger on his wife.
2 The aeroplane <u>left the ground</u> smoothly.
3 Your son <u>resembles</u> you in many ways.
4 If I were you I would <u>employ</u> more workers and finish the job quickly.
5 Don't let youself be <u>deceived</u> by appearances.
6 Philip is very popular with his classmates because he is clever at <u>mimicking</u>*the teachers.
7 I hope I haven't <u>occupied</u> too much of your time.
8 Her skirt was too loose and had to be <u>made narrower</u>.
9 I was so <u>surprised</u> by his reply that I couldn't say a word.
10 The newsreporters <u>recorded</u> the main points of the President's speech.
11 That large company has <u>assumed control of</u> many smaller ones.
12 The children <u>liked</u> the new maid immediately.

THINK

think about　　reflect upon
1 *vt insep*　　。。。のことを考える

　　I *have been thinking about* this all week, but I still can't understand it.
　　I *thought about* you all day, wondering what had happened to you.

think about　　consider; contemplate
2 *vt insep*　　検討する，。。。しようかと考える

　　Give me just a few more days *to think about* your offer.
　　I shall have *to think about* it carefully before I can give you a definite answer.
　　He *is thinking about* leaving his job and starting his own business.

think about　　have an opinion about
3 *vt insep*　　。。。のことを。。。と考える／思う

　　She doesn't seem to care what other people *think about* her.
　　Could you just look through this article and tell me what you *think about* it?

151

think back *vi*	turn the mind to past events 思い出す，思い起こす He *thought back* and tried to remember where he had seen that face before. Seeing those photographs made me *think back* to my early days in the army.
think of 1 *vt insep*	remember; recall 思い出す Can you *think of* the Japanese word for 'submarine'*? I know who you mean, but I can't *think of* his name at the moment. You *will think of* me sometimes, won't you?
think of 2 *vt insep*	consider; take into account 。。。のことを考える，思いやる He has his wife and family *to think of*. She never *thinks of* anyone but herself. I have other things *to think of*, you know!
think of 3 *vt insep*	plan to; contemplate 。。。しようかと思う Where *are* you *thinking of* going for your holidays this summer? I *did think of* phoning you at that late hour, but thought you might not like it. She *would* never *think of* marrying a horrible man like him.
think of 4 *vt insep*	have an opinion of 。。。のことを。。。と考える／思う What *do* you *think of* Omar Sharif as an actor? I don't *think* much *of* the so-called 'modern' art. His poetry *is* well *thought of* by the critics.
think of 5 *vt insep*	find; suggest 考え出す，思いつく We must *think of* some plan to get out of this place That's the only decent restaurant I can *think of* at the moment.

think of
6 vt insep

imagine
考えてみる，想像する

Think of all the time you have wasted!
Just *think of* the cost of a project like that!

think out
vt sep

plan by careful thinking
よく考えて計画を立てる

The assassin's* escape route *had been* carefully *thought out.*
The scheme seems *to be* well *thought out.*

think over
vt sep

consider at length
。。。のことをよく考える

We need a couple of days *to think over* your suggestions before we commit ourselves.
Please *think* this matter *over* and let me know your answer by Friday.

think up
vt sep

invent; concoct
(口実，案などを) 考え出す

Can't you *think up* some excuse to give him?
It's not always easy *to think up* original ideas.

EXERCISE 40

Fill in the blank spaces with the correct prepositions or particles:

1 Can you think ... the name of the first astronaut to land on the moon?
2 Just think ... all the money the government is spending on armament*.
3 She is very quick at thinking ... stories.
4 I don't know what to think ... this whole damned thing.
5 Your teachers obviously think very highly ... you.
6 The plot to depose* the king had been thoroughly thought ... by the conspirators*.
7 Think it ... and let me know what you decide.
8 Now think ..., Mrs Atkings, and see if you can remember anything at all that might help us find the murderer.
9 What were you thinking ... when I came in?
10 I just couldn't think ... harming that poor old lady.

THROW

throw about
vt sep*

throw here and there; scatter
投げ散らかす，浪費する

You mustn't *throw* litter *about* in the park.
He *is throwing* his money *about* like a madman.

throw away
1 *vt sep*

discard; dispose of
捨てる

We should *throw away* this table and buy a new one.
Don't *throw* those boxes *away*; they may come in handy* one day.

throw away
2 *vt sep*

let slip; miss
見逃す，棒に振る

You should never *have thrown away* such a good proposition*.
She had a marvellous opportunity to become an actress, but she *threw* it *away*.

throw in
1 *vt insep*

include without extra charge
おまけとして添える，サービスする

If you buy the house, we'll *throw in* the carpets.
He said I could have the scooter for only £30, with the helmet *thrown in*.

throw in
2 *vt sep*

interject
（ことばを）差しはさむ

He kept *throwing in* silly comments in spite of the chairman's warnings.

throw off
1 *vt sep*

remove hurriedly
急いで脱ぐ

She *threw off* her coat and shoes and lay down on the sofa.

throw off
2 *vt insep*

get rid of; free oneself from
。。。から免れる，捨てる，。。。との関係を絶つ

I don't seem to be able *to throw off* this wretched cold.
Throwing off all sense of pride, she begged him to marry her.
It is about time we *threw off* the yoke* of imperialism.

throw out
1 *vt sep*

expel; remove forcibly
追い出す，放校する，罷免する

The landlord threatened *to throw* her *out* if she didn't pay the rent.
He *has been thrown out* of college for bad conduct.

throw out
2 *vt insep*

emit; produce
(光熱を) 発する，出す

Coal fires don't always *throw out* much heat.
This small lamp *throws out* a very strong light.

throw out
3 *vt sep*

reject
否決する，拒否する

The board*of directors are inclined *to throw out* any proposals put forward by us.
The Bill *was thrown out* by a majority of 30 votes.

throw out
4 *vt sep*

= throw away (1)

throw over
vt sep

abandon; desert; forsake
見捨てる

She *threw over* her old friends when she won a fortune on the pools.
She *has thrown* her lover *over* for someone wealthier.

throw up
1 *vi, vt sep*

vomit; bring up
(食べた物を) 戻す，吐く

I can't eat anything: I feel like *throwing up*.
The sick child kept *throwing up* her food.

throw up
2 *vt sep*

abandon; give up
放棄する，やめる

She *threw up* her job to look after her ailing father. He *threw up* a promising career in the Foreign* Office to become a free-lance photographer.

EXERCISE 41

Fill in the blank spaces with the correct prepositions or particles:

1. Keep quiet, Sally, or I'll throw you . . . .
2. He threw . . . a good chance to compete in the Olympic Games.
3. He wouldn't stop throwing . . . all kinds of facetious* remarks.
4. Don't throw your books . . . in the room; the place looks terribly untidy.
5. I'll throw . . . two new tyres if you decide to buy the car.
6. That radiator doesn't throw . . . a lot of heat.
7. It would be foolish of you to throw . . . such a good job.
8. It took me more than a week to throw . . . that flu I had.
9. He threatened to kill his mistress if she threw him . . . .
10. He was terribly drunk and threw . . . everything he had eaten.

TURN

turn against
*vi, vt sep**

(cause to) become hostile to
。。。に対し反感を抱かせる

He had a strong feeling that all his friends *were turning against* him.
I will never forgive her for *turning* my own son *against* me.

turn (a) round
vi

face in the opposite direction
振り向く

She dared not *turn round* to see who was following her in the dark.

turn away
1 *vi*

look in a different direction
顔をそむける

She *turned away* in horror at the sight of her butchered husband.

156

turn away 2 *vt sep*	refuse admission or help to sb. 追い返す，引き返させる

These organizations seldom *turn away* anyone who is in dire* need of help.
As all tickets were sold out, many people had *to be turned away*.
I really hate *to turn* beggars *away*.

turn back 1 *vi, vt sep*	(cause to) go back 引き返す，追い返す，帰す，向きをかえる

Don't you think we should *turn back* now before the storm gets any worse?
The guards *turned* us *back* at the main gate.
They *turned* their car *back* and headed for safety.

turn back 2 *vt sep*	fold back 折り返す

She *turned back* the corner of the page to mark her place in the book.

turn down 1 *vt sep*	fold down 折りたたむ，折り返す

I wish you would stop this habit of *turning down* the pages of the book.

turn down 2 *vt sep*	lessen the intensity of; lower （火力，明るさ，音などを）小さくする

Don't forget *to turn down* the gas when the milk boils.
She *turned* the oil lamp *down*.

turn down 3 *vt sep*	refuse; reject 拒絶する，断わる

He did apply for that post, but they *turned* him *down*.
She *turned down* the job because it was badly paid.
His first book *was turned down* by a number of publishers.

turn in
1 vi

go to bed
床に入る

It was close upon midnight when we *turned in*.
It's time the children *were turning in*.

turn in
2 vt sep

surrender to the police
警察に引き渡す，届け出る

If we don't *turn* him *in* this time, the chances are he'll go on breaking the law.
She begged me not *to turn* her *in* and promised never to steal again.

turn inside out
vt sep*

reverse the sides; search thoroughly
裏返しになる，ひっくり返す

The strong wind *turned* her umbrella *inside out*.
The police *turned* the place *inside out* in search of the murder weapon.

turn into
vi, vt sep*

become; convert into
．．．になる，．．．に変える

A caterpillar ultimately *turns into* a butterfly or a moth.
Jesus is said *to have turned* water *into* wine.
We *are going to turn* the basement into a workshop.

turn off
1 vi, vt insep

branch off; change direction
道が分かれる，わき道へ入る

This is where the road to Lancaster *turns off*.
Turn off (the motorway) at the next exit.

turn off
2 vt sep

stop the flow of; switch off
（水道の水を）止める，（ガス，電気を）消す

You forgot *to turn off* the water in the bathroom.
Remember *to turn* the lights *off* before you go to bed.

turn off
3 vt sep*

cause to lose interest in
．．．に対する興味を失わせる，うんざりさせ

This kind of music really *turns* me *off*.

turn on
1 *vt sep*

start the flow of; switch on
（電気，ガスを）つける

I'll *turn on* the heater for a few minutes, if you don't mind.
Please *turn* the oven *on*; I'm going to bake some cakes.

turn on
2 *vt sep**

excite; stimulate
興奮させる

I think she is a great singer; she really *turns* the audience *on*.
That jazz sure *turns* me *on*, man!

turn on
3 *vt insep*

depend on
。。。しだいで定まる

The success of these talks *turns on* the willingness of both sides to make considerable concessions*.

turn on
4 *vt insep*

attack
襲いかかる

The dog *turned on* the postman and bit him in the thigh.

turn out
1 *vi*

assemble; gather
集まる

The whole village *turned out* to welcome the Queen.
In spite of the cold weather, thousands of people *turned out* to see the Grand* National.

turn out
2 *vi*

prove to be; transpire
。。。とわかる

He *turned out* to be a thoroughly dishonest person.
The project *turned out* (to be) a complete failure.
It *turned out* that he was a Russian spy.

turn out
3 *vt sep*

evict; expel
追い出す

Her landlord *turned* her *out* for not paying the rent.
Turn those children *out* of my study, will you?

turn out
4 *vt sep*

clean thoroughly; empty
(中の物を外へ出して）掃除する，空にする

My mother *turns out* the bedrooms once a week.
He *turned* his pockets *out* in search of his train ticket.

turn out
5 *vt sep*

extinguish
消す

Don't forget *to turn out* the lights before you go out.

turn over
1 *vi*

capsize; overturn
ひっくり返る

The small rowing-boat *turned over* in the gale.
The car hit a lamp-post and *turned over*.

turn over
2 *vi, vt sep*

change sides; invert
向きを変える，ひっくり返す

He couldn't sleep last night and kept *turning over* in bed.
Nobody could *turn over* that big stone.
Will you help me *turn* the mattress *over*, please?

turn over
3 *vt insep*

do business to the amount of
。。。の商売をする

We *turned over* no less than a million pounds last year.

turn over
4 *vt sep*

deliver; hand over
引き渡す

They *turned* the escaped prisoner *over* to the police
You did the right thing in *turning* him *over* to the authorities.

turn to
vt insep

go to (for help, advice, etc.)
(。。。に救い，助言を）求める

She has no one *to turn to* for advice, poor thing!
He always *turns to* me when he is in trouble.

turn up
1 *vi*

arrive; come
来る

I waited for him for nearly one hour, but he did not *turn up*.
Only half the members *turned up* at last night's meeting.

turn up
2 *vi*

come to light; be found
出てくる，現われる

These things always *turn up* when you don't need them.
Please don't worry about my lighter; it'*ll turn up* eventually.

turn up
3 *vi*

happen; occur
起こる

If anything *turns up*, I'll let you know.
Something is bound *to turn up* sooner or later.

turn up
4 *vt sep*

cause to face upwards
立てる

She *turned up* the collar of her coat against the cold wind.

turn up
5 *vt sep*

find; discover
見つける

You can always *turn up* his address in the telephone directory.
We *have turned up* some information that may interest you.

turn up
6 *vt sep*

increase the intensity of (cf: *turn down*)
(ガスなどを) 強くする，(音を) 大きくする

Will you *turn up* the radio, John? I can hardly hear a thing.
Turn up the gas just a little bit.

161

turn upside down
vt sep*

invert; search thoroughly
さかさまにする，探すのに（場所を）
めちゃくちゃにする

You've *turned* the painting *upside down*, haven't you?
He *turned* the whole piace *upside down*, looking for his boots.

EXERCISES 42

A Fill in the blank spaces with the correct prepositions or particles. In some examples more than one answer is possible:

1 I haven't found a job yet, but I hope something will turn ... soon.
2 Turn your collar ... ; it's sticking up at the back.
3 Do you mind turning ... the wireless? It's making too much noise.
4 He never lets down anyone who turns ... him for help.
5 That shop turns ... something like a thousand pounds a day.
6 The oil tanker caught fire and turned ... an inferno*.
7 Turn ... the television if you are not watching it.
8 Thieves broke into the shop and turned everything ....
9 Turn ... the light, please; it's getting dark in here.
10 A large crowd turned ... to welcome the president.

B Replace the underlined words with phrasal verbs containing *turn*:

1 We <u>went to bed</u> rather late last night.
2 The small boat <u>capsized</u> in the storm.
3 A lot of people <u>had to be refused admission to</u> the concert-hall.
4 We agreed to be there at eight, but he <u>arrived</u> one hour later.
5 The bull <u>attacked</u> the matador and knocked him senseless.
6 The exam <u>proved</u> to be much easier than we had expected.
7 Everything <u>depends on</u> what happens next.
8 The director <u>refused his</u> request for a transfer to headquarters.
9 He was <u>expelled from</u> the club because he did not have a membership card.

WEAR

wear away
vi, vt sep

(cause to) disappear or become thin through friction etc.
摩滅する，すりへらす

The inscription* on the monument *has worn away* and can scarcely be read.
The waves *had worn away* the cliffs.
Wind and rain *have worn* these rocks *away*.

wear down
1 *vi, vt sep*

(cause to) become smaller by rubbing or use
すりへる，すりへらす

The heels of your shoes *are* quickly *wearing down*.
The heels of your shoes *are* badly *worn down*.
These rough roads *will* soon *wear down* the tyres of your car.

wear down
2 *vt sep*

weaken by constant pressure or attack
疲れさせる，弱らせる

They have at last succeeded in *wearing down* the opposition.
The two boxers were trying *to wear* each other *down*.

wear off
vi

disappear; pass away
消え去る

The public will forget all about this incident as soon as the novelty* *wears off*.
I'm glad your headache *is wearing off*.

wear on
vi

pass slowly or tediously
(時が) 経つ

As the day *wore on*, she became more and more anxious.
Several months *wore on* and nothing was heard of him.

wear out
1 *vi, vt sep*

(cause to) become useless through wear
すりへる，使い古す

Children's shoes *wear out* very quickly.
Most of the machines in this factory *are wearing out*.
Children *wear out* their shoes very quickly.
This old jacket *is* almost *worn out*.

wear out
2 *vt sep*

exhaust; tire out
疲れ果てる

I don't want you *to wear* yourself *out* like that.
What's the matter, Nick? You look utterly *worn out*.

EXERCISE 43

Fill in the blank spaces with the correct prepositions or particles:
1. She was completely worn ... after a long, busy day.
2. Everyone was growing restless as the evening wore ... and nothing happened.
3. Cheap clothes do not necessarily wear ... more quickly than expensive ones.
4. Her shyness will probably wear ... when she gets to know you better.
5. You'll have to wear this coat ... before I can buy you a new one.
6. You should sharpen your pencil; the point is quite worn ....
7. The feet of so many tourists had worn ... the steps.
8. We must wear ... the enemy's resistance at all costs.

WORK

work at
vt insep

apply oneself to; be busy at
専念する

You've got *to work at* your German if you want to have a chance of passing the exam.
I *have been working at* this essay all week.

work in(to)
vt sep

introduce
入れる，交える

His lectures wouldn't be so dull if he could *work in* a bit of humour.
He always manages *to work* politics *into* the conversation.

work off
1 *vt sep*

get rid of, free oneself of (a debt)
(負債を) 働いて返済する

By this time next year I *will have worked off* all my debts.

work off
2 *vt sep*

give expression to, vent
(うっぷんなどを) 晴らす

She *worked off* her anger on the poor dog.

work on
1 *vt insep*

be engaged in
。。。に従事する

We *are working on* a slightly different project at present.
What exactly *is* he *working on* for his doctorate?

work on 2 *vt insep*	seek to persuade or influence sb. 説得に努める He won't let me do it unless you *work on* him. I don't promise you anything, but I shall certainly *work on* him.
work out 1 *vi*	develop in a certain way 。。。になる，うまくいく Things did not quite *work out* the way we had hoped. Everything *worked out* all right in the end.
work out 2 *vi*	train oneself physically 練習する The athletes *worked out* for five hours a day before the Olympics.
work out 3 *vi, vt sep*	estimate; calculate 見積もる，計算する We *worked out* that it would cost £300 to instal a central-heating system. I'*ll have to work out* the cost of this trip to see if we can afford it.
work out 4 *vt sep*	solve 解く I can't *work out* these difficult equations*. Have you *worked out* this puzzle yet?
work out 5 *vt sep*	devise; plan 細かく立てる，立案する I think we ought to wait until we *have worked out* a plan of campaign. It seems to be a well *worked-out* scheme.
work out 6 *vt sep*	exhaust (a mine) (鉱山を) 堀り尽くす Those coalmines are now completely *worked out*.

165

work out at *vt insep*	amount to （金額が）．．．となる	

His fees *work out at* forty pounds a day.
What does your share of the profits *work out at*?

work up 1 *vt sep*	arouse; excite 興奮させる	

The speaker *was working up* the crowd into an absolute frenzy*.
Oh, you *do work* yourself *up* over nothing.
What's she so *worked up* about?

work up 2 *vt sep*	develop; build up 築き上げる，（素材を）．．．に作り上げる	

My brother and I *worked up* the business from nothing.
I might try *to work up* these notes into a small book.

work up 3 *vt sep*	stimulate; arouse （興味，食欲などを）ひき起こす	

So far we haven't been able *to work up* any enthusiasm for the scheme.
A brisk* walk in the park *will work up* your appetite.

work up to 1 *vt insep*	rise gradually to ．．．に進む，しだいに．．．になる	

The story *works up to* a thrilling climax.

work up to 2 *vt insep*	prepare the way for 作り上げる	

What exactly *are* you *working up to*?

EXERCISE 44

Use synonyms in place of the underlined phrasal verbs:

1 He seems to be fond of working quotations* into his speeches.
2 Please don't work your bad temper off on me.
3 He certainly knows how to work up an audience.
4 Skiing isn't easy; you've got to work at it.
5 Can you work out how long it will take us to get to Hull from here?

6 He is now working on a new novel.
7 You should be able to work out this problem in a couple of minutes.
8 Scientists have recently worked out a new method of measuring the depths of the oceans.
9 We have worked up a great deal of interest in your campaign.
10 The bill works out at five pounds each.

ENGLISH – JAPANESE GLOSSARY

The page reference given indicates the place where the word first occurs in the text. Each word translated in the glossary is marked with an asterisk (*) in the text.

下のページ表示は、本書においてその語が初めて出てくる箇所を記している。 これらグロッサリーの単語は、文中において、星印 * が付けられている。

abbreviation, p. 142	略語
abide by, p. 10	守る
abolition, p. 12	廃止
abortive, p. 29	失敗に終わる
A.D. (Anno Domini), p. 142	キリスト紀元（西暦...年）
adequate, p. 53	適切な
affair, have an ___ with, p. 54	...と関係をもつ
agenda, p. 79	会議事項
ailment, p. 84	軽い病気
air-raid, p. 63	空襲の
allegations, p. 28	（証拠のない）申し立て
amid, p. 68	...の中に
ammunition, p. 62	弾薬
antagonize, p. 85	反感をかう
anticipate, p. 52	予想する
appendix, p. 148	虫垂
applause, p. 68	拍手かっさい
appreciably, p. 51	かなり
armament, p. 153	軍備
arrogant, p. 150	横柄な

arthritis, p. 83	関節炎
artillery, p. 27	砲兵
assassin, p. 153	暗殺者
assault, p. 116	暴行を加える
attribute, ___to, p. 123	。。。のためだとする
auditor, p. 72	会計検査官
back-bencher, p. 28	評議員
ban, p. 117	禁止
bandit, p. 53	追いはぎ
bank on, p. 59	。。。にたよる
bankrupt, go __, p. 78	破産する
beleaguered, p. 79	包囲された
benefactor, p. 122	後援者
bereavement, p. 17	先立たれること
besieged, p. 62	攻囲された
bickering, p. 52	口論
Bill, p. 24	議案
binoculars, p. 100	双眼鏡
blackmail, p. 62	恐かつ
blood donor, p. 76	給血者
board of directors, the __, p. 155	理事会
brag, p. 145	自慢する
brisk, p. 166	元気のよい
brochure, p. 75	パンフレット
budget, p. 129	予算
building society, p. 110	住宅金融共済組合
bully, p. 143	乱暴者

burglar, p. 20	強盗
butler, p. 137	執事
capital punishment, p. 23	死刑
capsize, p. 18	(船が) ひっくり返る
casualties, p. 63	死傷者
commandos, p. 18	選抜攻撃隊
commission, p. 136	委員会
commute, p. 133	減刑する
comply with, p. 10	従う
concessions, p. 159	譲歩
conspirator, p. 153	共謀者
contemporary, p. 141	同年者
controversy, p. 134	論争
convert, p. 145	変える
convict, p. 58	囚人
convoy, p. 53	護衛団
corporal punishment, p. 27	体罰
corpse, p. 90	死体
corrupt, p. 90	腐敗する
corruption, p. 28	汚職
crook, p. 91	詐欺師
culprit, p. 95	犯人
death penalty, p. 12	死刑
debris, p. 34	破片
decamp, p. 106	逃亡する
decipher, p. 106	判読する

defective, p. 29	欠陥のある
delegation, p. 15	代表派遣団
depose, p. 153	退位させる
depression, p. 89	不況
derelict, p. 112	遺棄された
destiny, p. 25	運命
deteriorate, p. 44	悪化する
diagnosis, p. 13	診断
dire, in __need of help, p. 157	至急救助を要する
disabled, the __, p. 61	身体障害者
disarray, in __, p. 50	入り乱れて
discern, p. 106	はっきり見る
discretion, p. 96	慎重さ
dissertation, p. 128	論文
dogged, p. 21	根気強い
doth, p. 90	(古) do の三人称単数直説法現在形
draft dodger, p. 37	徴兵忌避者
draught, = draft, p. 83	すきま風
drench, p. 38	びしょぬれになる
drive, p. 98	気力
drought, p. 24	ひでり
dull-witted, p. 146	頭の鈍い
electorate, p. 115	有権者
enthusiasm, p. 30	熱中
epidemic, p. 21	流行病
equation, p. 165	方程式
expenditure, p. 78	支出

facetious, p. 156	おどけた
fanatic, p. 47	狂信者
fancy-dress ball, p. 61	仮装舞踏会
feign, p. 58	。。。のふりをする
ferocity, p. 117	残忍な行為
fine, p. 57	罰金
fishy, p. 71	怪しい
Foreign Office, p. 156	（英国）外務省
fossil, p. 136	化石
frenzy, p. 166	逆上
fugitive, p. 64	逃亡者
fumes, p. 63	（悪臭のある有害な）煙霧
garment, p. 92	衣服
garrison, p. 78	守備隊
Grand National, the __, p. 159	グランドナショナル（Liverpoolで毎年行われる4½マイルの大障害競馬）
grant, p. 141	奨学金
heckler, p. 20	（弁士を）やじり倒す人
heiress, p. 35	女性の相続人
hitch, without a __, p. 71	滞りなく
Home Secretary, p. 28	内相
hooligan, p. 137	不良
illicit, p. 25	不法な
impertinence, p. 122	ずうずうしさ
imposter, p. 138	詐欺師

impression, p. 126	（印刷）原版の...刷り
impudence, p. 17	厚かましさ
indecent exposure, p. 126	わいせつ罪
indignation, p. 82	憤り
indispensable, p. 124	絶対必要な
inferno, p. 162	（大火災などの）地獄のような場所
infidelity, p. 109	不貞
inscription, p. 162	碑文
instalment, p. 50	分割払い込み金
intimidation, p. 141．	脅迫
intruder, p. 69	侵入者
invigilator, p. 63	試験監督者
jubilant, p. 81	（歓声をあげて）喜ぶ
jury, p. 24	陪審
laughing stock, p. 56	物笑いの種
lay-by, p. 112	待避場所
League of Nations, the ＿, p. 137	国際連盟
leak, spring a ＿, p. 69	漏り始める
leeway, p. 105	（時間，金などの）余裕
loot, p. 22	略奪する
lot, a bad ＿, p. 150	評判のよくない悪いやつ
magistrate, p. 94	軽罪判事
malnutrition, p. 20	栄養不良
matador, p. 69	闘牛の主役

mimick, p. 151	...の物まねをする
minutes, p. 30	議事録
moaning, p. 43	うめき声
moth, p. 90	(こん虫)衣が
M.P. (Member of Parliament), p. 23	(英)国会議員
naivety, p. 46	純真
napping, be caught __, p. 41	油断に乗じられる
neck, stick one's __out, p. 147	自ら身を危険にさらす
nomads, p. 51	遊牧民
novelty, p. 163	珍しさ
obstacle, p. 129	障害物
obstinate, p. 143	がんこな
office, p. 39	公職
opponent, p. 88	(勝負, 議論などの) 相手
Opposition leader, p. 78	反対党のリーダー
ordeal, p. 32	苦しい体験
ornithology, p. 41	鳥類学
outdated, p. 47	時代遅れの
outlaw, p. 149	追放者
outrageous, p. 80	乱暴な
outstanding, p. 110	未決着の
overdue, p. 30	返却期限の過ぎた
penalize, p. 10	罰する
permissive society, p. 78	(性などについて) 寛大な社会

petty cash, p. 52	小口現金
petty thief, p. 94	こそ泥
pincers, p. 113	くぎ抜き
plead with, p. 64	嘆願する
pneumonia, p. 25	肺炎
poke, p. 71	(火を棒などで）かきたてる
precision, p. 41	精密
prejudices, p. 91	偏見
premier, p. 75	首相
premises, p. 130	家屋敷
prescription, make up __, p. 105	処方せんの調剤をする
prey, p. 16	えじき
procession, p. 29	行列
proposition, p. 154	提案
provisions, p. 79	食料
provocative, p. 82	挑発的な
quid, p. 137	(俗語) 1 ポンド
quotation, p. 166	引用
ransack, p. 20	あさりまわる
rashness, p. 110	無謀
rebellious, p. 85	反抗的な
recklessly, p. 60	むてっぽうに
reconciliation, p. 23	和解
reconnaissance, p. 27	偵察
refinery, oil __, p. 18	精油所

reform, p. 24	改正
regiment, p. 43	連隊
reinforcements, p. 79	増援隊
renovate, p. 50	修繕する
repel, p. 123	追い払う
reserved, p. 49	無口な
reservist, p. 29	予備兵
resignation, p. 55	辞職
resume, p. 19	再開する
reviewer, p. 44	（新刊書などの）批評家
revolt, p. 117	暴動
rich food, p. 42	こってりした食べ物
rogue, p. 142	ごろつき
row, p. 151	けんか
ruthlessly, p. 78	乱暴に
scaffolding, p. 145	足場
seamstress, p. 44	針子
sedative, p. 96	鎮静剤
sentry, p. 128	歩しょう
shoelaces, p. 46	くつひも
shrewd, p. 33	賢い
skid, p. 129	横すべりする
squalid, p. 27	ごみごみした
stationary, p. 126	止まっている
stray, p. 146	道に迷った
stuff, p. 54	学科
surrender, p. 43	降参する

surveyor, p. 100	鑑定人
suspect, p. 72	容疑者
synonym, p. 18	同義語
tax evasion, p. 27	脱税
through thick and thin, p. 140	終始変わらずに
tissue, p. 41	（生物体の）組織
Tories, the __, p. 57	英国の保守党
track down, p. 66	追い詰める
traffic jam, p. 77	交通渋滞
traitor, p. 99	反逆者
trespasser, p. 83	不法侵入者
trivial, p. 52	つまらない
truancy, p. 64	無断欠席
Tube, the __, p. 41	ロンドンの地下鉄
undertaker, p. 90	葬儀屋
unemployment benefit, p. 111	失業手当
vacuum cleaner, p. 47	電気掃除機
verdict, p. 24	評決
vicious, p. 20	癖の悪い
virtue, by __ of, p. 141	･･･のお陰で
window-sill, p. 97	窓下の横材
wistfully, p. 102	なつかしそうに
withstand, p. 142	耐える
yoke of imperialism, p. 155	帝政の束縛
zebra crossing, p. 49	横断歩道